RIVER

SNAKE RIVER

G   O   N

Adapted from the map
in Bancroft's HISTORY
OF OREGON, v. 1, San
Francisco, 1886, whose
inaccuracies are not
significant for the
setting of this story.

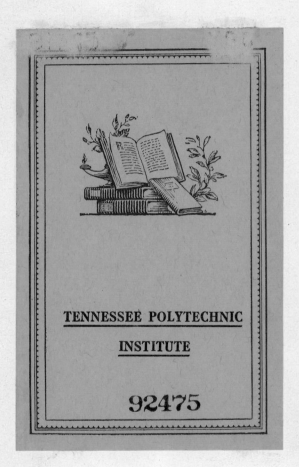

AN OREGON IDYL

By Nellie May Young

A tale of a transcontinental journey, and life in Oregon in 1883-1884, based on the Diary of Janette Lewis Young

"For life, with all it yields of joy and woe
And hope and fear,
Is just our chance o' the prize of learning love,
How love might be, hath been indeed, and is."

ROBERT BROWNING

THE ARTHUR H. CLARK COMPANY
GLENDALE, CALIFORNIA
1961

92475

Printed by DAPCO - 8, Via Dandolo - Rome, Italy

William Stewart Young, at time of graduation from
Union Theological Seminary, 1883.

Contents

Foreword

To all who may have the good fortune to hold this book in their hands, with some time available for leisurely reading, I take great pleasure in introducing the author — Mrs. Nellie May Young, the wife of Arthur N. Young, a son of Dr. William Stewart Young by his second marriage. By a curious set of circumstances, which Mrs. Young relates in her preface, the original Diary of Janette Lewis Young disappeared from the office of the Presbyterian Headquarters in Los Angeles and was offered for sale some time later at the Presbyterian Headquarters in San Francisco. Also, by another curious set of circumstances, on a Sunday afternoon several years ago, I called at the Arthur N. Young home in San Marino, while looking for the home of a Mr. Jung (pronounced "Young"), who I thought lived on the same street. In the introductions that followed, I learned that Arthur N. Young was the son of William Stewart Young. I then announced: "We have the original Young Diary at the Seminary." Mr. Arthur N. Young then claimed: "No, we have the original Diary." Later upon examining the original documents, we found that he had in mind a partial Diary kept by his mother; and that the family had no knowledge of that kept by Janette Lewis Young.

Thus it happened that Mrs. Nellie May Young had the opportunity to examine the Diary of Mrs. Janette Lewis Young. She was so inspired by the unfolding story of the young couple who went to the home mission field in Oregon during the early 1880's, and by the charming descriptions of frontier life, that she was moved to give this story to the public under the title, An Oregon Idyl. Since so very few works of this nature, or dealing with this period, have been published, I hail this particular book with joy. The experiences and contributions of our forefathers in the faith here on the Pacific Slope should not be forgotten.

Furthermore, this volume is important because of the light it throws upon the life of one of the most influential Presbyterian ministers in the history of California—William Stewart Young.

May this book, An Oregon Idyl, find a large reading public and thus keep green the memory of two unusually fine people — William Stewart Young and Janette Lewis Young.

CLIFFORD M. DRURY

San Francisco Theological Seminary
    San Anselmo, California

Preface

This book is based on the Diary of Janette Lewis Young. She and her husband, the Reverend William Stewart Young, travelled from Pennsylvania to Oregon in June, 1883. He had just graduated from Union Theological Seminary in New York, and had been appointed a Home Missionary under the Presbyterian Board.

They spent about a year and a half in Oregon. In December, 1884, they had to go to California for Janette's health. For a time she was better, and continued her interest in church work. But, afflicted with tuberculosis, her health slowly failed, and death came at Los Angeles, October 26, 1887, at the age of 29.

Settling in Los Angeles, William Stewart Young soon became prominent in religious, educational and civic activities. After his death in 1937, Janette's Diary was among the papers turned over to Dr. Thomas Holden and Dr. Glenn Moore, his successors in California Presbyterian work. Relating to a closed chapter of his life, the Diary was unknown to his family. Mysteriously it disapppeared from Dr. Moore's office in Los Angeles. Sometime later it was among papers tendered to Dr. Clyde Smith, of the Presbyterian office in San Francisco, by a rough-looking man who said he had found them in a trash can and had recognized them as being Presbyterian. He wanted money for the papers, but Dr. Smith refused to pay, and, giving the man a quarter, ushered him out of his office. Dr. Smith turned over the Diary to Professor Clifford M. Drury, of San Francisco Theological Seminary, who deposited it in the Seminary's Library.

William Stewart Young, I think, spoke more freely of Janette to me, his daughter-in-law, than to his children. None of us ever saw Janette's picture; but I have a vivid impression of her from Father's descriptions. She was obviously a young woman of intelligence, perception, humor and courage — as this story will show.

The descriptive material in this book is mostly paraphrased from or based upon the Diary, with some use of other contemporary data. The same is true of the conversation, which is what the record shows could well have been said. There is no element of fiction, in the sense of departing from the record and the facts or of changing the characters of those mentioned.

I am much indebted to Professor Clifford M. Drury of San Francisco Theological Seminary, to Dr. John E. Pomfret, Director of the Huntington Library, and to Mr. Alfred Powers, of Portland, Oregon, for reading the manuscript and making valuable suggestions. Mrs. Harris Ball kindly helped with proof-reading, and Mr. Charles Tidball both helped with proof-reading and gave invaluable aid in seeing the manuscript through the press. My husband, Arthur N. Young, helped in many ways, and his sister, Sarah Adele Young, painstakingly prepared the manuscript for publication.

N. M. Y.

I. On Unknown Paths

The conductor of the Pennsylvania Limited Express was decidedly out of sorts that noon of June 18, 1883. He had not wanted to stop at the little one-horse town of Parkesburg, 45 miles west of Philadelphia, but the station master had telegraphed the request to Philadelphia and orders were orders.

"All aboard," he shouted impatiently, cutting short Janette's and Will's tearful farewell with their loved ones. They got on board and went out to the rear of the last car, as the engineer blew his whistle and the train started with a jerk.

There at the station stood Father and Mother Young, sisters Fannie and Clara, Janette's Father and Mother Lewis, her sister Annie and her younger brother Clifford. They and many others from the Upper Octorara Presbyterian Church had come to the train to see them off. Their voices blended in the song, "God be with you till we meet again."

As the train gathered speed they turned for one last look at the Young farm, "Fairview." There were the big stone barns and the pastures for Father's horses and cattle. Next winter he would care for Buffalo Bill Cody's horses, after the "Wild West Show" had ended its fall tour of the East. There too was the spring-house in the shade of the willow tree, where Sister Clara skimmed the cream from the milk in the shiny tin pans and churned it into butter. Farther up the hill was the old stone house, with the date "1820" over the door. Built by Grandfather Thomas Young, it was sturdy enough to last for generations. As the train sped on, past familiar landmarks, Janette choked back her tears. Seeing that no one was looking, Will put his arm around her and kissed her tenderly.

They turned and walked through the cars until they found their red plush-covered seats in the Pullman car. They were lucky to have a lower berth, for which they had paid three dollars extra. They were met by smiles from other passengers. Janette blushed and whispered to Will, "Do you suppose they think we are a honeymoon couple?"

"How could they?," Will replied, but his eyes had a mischievous twinkle.

What the passengers saw as the young couple came down the aisle was a serious young man loaded with satchels and valises, followed by his charming wife. Her silver grey dress fitted snugly across her bosom, while her skirt billowed out in back over a stylish bustle. Her grey bonnet trimmed with purple pansies rested on her brown hair, and was tied under her chin sedately with velvet ribbons—but she was quite unaware that Will's hurried embrace had tipped the bonnet at a rakish angle over one ear, and Will, man-like, had not noticed it.

When they reached their seats she removed her bonnet and settled down to enjoy the trip. As the porter helped them stow their luggage under the seats and put their wraps in the rack above, he asked, "Is you folks jes' married?"

"Goodness no!," and Janette blushed even more. Then to Will she whispered, "I wish I would get over this silly habit of blushing. I am really used to being Mrs. Young by this time."

His smile reassured her, "Blushing, you know, is very becoming to you."

By then they had been married for over a month. He had accepted a call from the Presbyterian Board to go as a home missionary to the Willamette Valley, Oregon, and now they were off on their long journey to the far west. They had been childhood schoolmates and sweethearts living on adjoining farms. While he was at Lafayette College and Union Theological Seminary they had corresponded, and he knew that she was the one girl in the world for him. Janette had always adored him. She had taught school while he was in the Seminary. It had been a proud day for her when in April Will was ordained to the ministry at Oxford, Pennsylvania, by the Presbytery of Chester. It was natural for him to want to enter the ministry, since two of his seven uncles on his father's side were ministers. They often visited in his home, and encouraged him to follow in their footsteps.

On hearing that he was to be married, one of Will's thrifty Quaker cousins had given him the following bit of advice:

"Don't thee wed for money, friend,
For money hath a sting.
Don't thee wed a pretty face
'Tis but a foolish thing;

Don't thee wed for place nor fame,
'Twill disappoint thy hope,
But when thee marries, choose a girl
Who uses Ivory soap.
It floats."

Luckily Janette could qualify in that respect.

In her Diary, Janette describes her wedding and honeymoon:
May 16.

"On May 11, 1883, Miss H. Janette Lewis and W. S. Young were united in matrimony by Rev. Joel S. Gilfillan assisted by Rev. James Marshall. Revs. E. R. Murgatroyd, I. F. King, E. D. Van Dyck, and W. S. Barnes had come on from New York. They acted as ushers together with M. G. Simpson, A. T. Parke and C. W. Lewis.

"Rev. H. S. Dickey and Miss Annie Snead were the only waiters.

"In the morning of the day—Friday, to which everybody said was so unlucky a day and nobody but Willie Young and Jennie Lewis would have courage to face the talk such a day for a wedding would create, at 9 o'clock a breakfast was served at Thorndale to which only near relatives and friends were invited. It was 11:30 ere we left the house and to drive ten miles and be on hand at 1 required fast driving. But we reached the church before time and found a large number of people there. The body of the church well filled. Miss Annie H. Boyd played Mendel [How do you spell it? It was unthinkable for a school teacher not to know, so there it remains unfinished] and all passed off pleasantly, though Joel listened sharp for the 'Yes' to the 'Obey' and though the ring did not slip on as easy as grease."

In describing the wedding the Parkesburg paper, under the title of "The Silken Tie," said:

"The bride was becomingly attired in a silver grey travelling dress with cape. Jessamine flowers, which were sent by a friend in Florida expressly for the occasion, added much to the beautiful appearance of the young lady."

They made an attractive couple as they stood there in the Upper Octorara Presbyterian Church to be joined in marriage. Janette was twenty-four and Will was nearing his twenty-fourth birthday. Her dark hair was arranged in curls over her forehead. She had a small straight nose, warm brown eyes under dark eyebrows, and long curling lashes. She was slender and almost as tall as Will, who was of medium height, blond and blue-eyed, with soft flowing side whiskers. As he pledged his troth he looked earnestly at the face of his lovely bride, who gave him a radiant smile.

The Diary continues:

"After the ceremony we stopped in the vestibule a few minutes and held an informal reception mainly for those who had come from so many different directions to the church and who would not likely see us again. Then we drove to the train and were off for Philadelphia and New York at 2 P.M.

"At New York we stopped at the St. Stephens. Saturday we spent buying a piano, viewing obelisk, Central Park, museums, art galleries, and view from Domestic building and in the eve we rested; Sunday we went to hear Dr. Parkhurst. Monday morn we walked over Brooklyn Bridge [It had just been finished but not formally opened to traffic] went to Bulls and Bears and then returned to hotel and 4 P.M. left for Philadelphia and thence to Thorndale and on Tuesday morn. to Parkesburg and after dinner we drove to Cochranville to attend the wedding of Hervey Dickey and Annie Snead. Rev. J. A. Watson performed the ceremony assisted by Rev. J. S. Gilfillan and W. S. Young. We accompanied them to the train and then went home."

And again on June 18th:

"From the 18th of May till 18th of June we rested and visited our friends and packed our goods — attended receptions, suppers, etc. until June 18th when we started for Oregon wondering much what the great wide West had in store for us and what would be the changes ere we saw the home faces again. We left Parkesburg at 1 o'clock on the limited express which had been telegraphed to stop."

Will had gone to Colorado in the summer of 1881, and had preached in the Presbyterian churches of Greeley and Boulder. So he felt like a seasoned traveller. To help plan their trip West, he had brought home from New York a book called, "The Pacific Tourist," by F. E. Shearer, Editor, published in New York the year before. He read several passages to Janette, to impress her with the pleasures of travel:

"In no place can travel be so easy as on the Pacific Railway.

One lives at home in the Palace car. In one week the train will leisurely cross the continent. The little section and berth allotted to you, so clean and neat, becomes your home. Here you sit and read and play games or enjoy conversation. As far as Chicago the trains rush along at forty miles an hour and you have no time to enjoy Pullman car life. But once you cross the Mississippi the pace becomes more leisurely.

"When night comes and your little berth is made up, you snugly cover under double blankets, for the night air is crisp and cool, then rest sweetly and refreshingly as ever in your bed at home. How little has been written about the delightful, snug, rejuvenating sleep on the Pacific Railroad."

This all sounded very well, but Janette found it less delightful than it was described. The humor of the time reflected the public's feeling about the various lines. Thus the D.L. & W. (Delaware, Lackawanna and Western) was the "Delay, Linger and Wait." The N.D. & C. (Newburgh, Duchess and Connecticut) was the "Never Did and Couldn't." And the C.B. and Q. R.R. (Chicago, Burlington and Quincy Railroad) was the "Come, Boys, and Quit Railroading."

"We are lucky," Will remarked, "to be travelling now instead of 20 years ago, when Uncle John made a trip to Chicago. He told me that in those days a night journey was something to be dreaded. The passengers lay down, fully dressed, on rough mattresses and put their overcoats and shawls over them. Candles furnished the light, and heat came from wood- or coal-burning stoves."

Summer was at its best, and through the fertile farmlands of Pennsylvania the fields were green with hay and corn, while the orchards were heavy with fruit. The houses built of stone were well kept and attractive, surrounded by trees, shrubbery and bright colored flowers. The immense white-washed barns, facing the south, so characteristic of Pennsylvania, and the green pastures where grazed the cattle and the horses, all told of the thrift of the owners. They watched the ever changing view from their car windows, and recalled the events of the past month and enjoyed the novelty and excitement of their transcontinental journey.

About 5:30 Janette got out the lunch basket, and Will rang for the porter to bring a table and put it up for them. Sisters Fannie and Clara had packed their basket carefully with sandwiches, fried chicken, deviled eggs, angel food cake and other delicacies. Janette's mother had added homemade pickles, crab-apple jelly and fruit.

They had good appetites, as it had been a long time since dinner. Also, because of the prospect of leaving, they had been too excited to eat very much. They saved some for the next day.

Some trains, but not theirs, carried a "hotel car," as the diners were called. Their motto was, "Eat and be satisfied. Meals are served in first class style. Passengers appreciate this new feature of 'Life on the Road'."

Janette's Diary of June 18 continues:

"We reached Huntington [Pennsylvania] at six at which we were delayed a few minutes by a wreck. Here we began to enjoy the mountain scenery."

When the train had stopped so suddenly they were anxious and wondered what had happened. After some delay the train started again slowly, and they learned that a freight train ahead of them had run into a farm wagon. They were glad to learn that no one was hurt, but they felt sorry for the farmer as they inched slowly ahead and saw the piles of fruit and vegetables scattered along the track.

As dusk came on, the train began climbing the gently rolling hills. Lights began to glow in the houses and smoke was coming from the chimneys.

The dimly lighted stations and straggling towns slipped by them in the darkness, with fields and woods between. The deserted stations gave them a feeling of sadness. They felt they were saying farewell to Pennsylvania and the way of life they had known.

The Diary goes on:

"Reached Altoona [Pennsylvania] at 8 P.M. and it was too dark to see the mountains. Horseshoe Bend merits its name, being night though we could only judge of it from the lights that were as guides to the engines."

Janette had never spent a night on the train, and when the colored porter started to make up the beds, she watched him with interest. First he moved the seats and let the backs down to form the bed, then he pulled down the upper berth and took from it the mattress. Then came the long slabs of board that formed the partitions between the berths. She was pleased to see that the bed linen was clean and fresh.

"Oh, Will," Janette complained, "how am I ever going to manage to undress in this crowded space?"

Will laughed. "Well dear, I guess there is nothing for you to

If you ladies didn't wear so many
_r."

am certainly glad that we spent our
ad of starting out immediately for the
ey Dickey."

bag of toilet articles, Janette made her
way to the ___ ___ ___, in the rear of the car. In the corridor
she had to stand in line w.. h four or five other women waiting their
turn. What irked them was that the porter came by and locked
the door and kept it locked until they passed Johnstown [Penn-
sylvania], for fear that someone would flush the toilet while the
train was standing in the station.

When she finally got into the little washroom it was so small
that she could barely turn around. The swaying motion of the train
made washing so difficult that she just gave her face a "lick and a
promise." She was glad that she had brought her own sponge,
towel and soap; for by the end of the day there was hardly a clean
spot left on the roller towel. When she was finally ready, she
started back to her berth. Seeing the long line of green baize curtains all looking alike, she became panic-stricken for a minute. What
was the number of their berth? She couldn't remember. Just then
Will's blond head appeared, as he put out his shoes for the porter
to polish, and she was greatly relieved.

Then came the struggle to get undressed in the berth, in which
she could barely sit upright. She had to remove her grey silk
travelling dress, several muslin petticoats, trimmed with embroidery
and hand-crocheted lace, then her bustle which was strapped about
her waist, a voluminous pair of lace-trimmed drawers, and a corset
cover. It was with great difficulty that she took off her corset and
then her chemise. By the time she had put on her white muslin
night-gown, trimmed with hand-crocheted lace, she felt quite worn
out. Finally, off came her high buttoned black shoes and black
stockings that were held up with blue round garters.

Will meantime had a much easier time of it. He put his watch
and wallet inside the pillow, lest they be stolen in the night through
the curtains. After he took off his coat, vest and trousers and hung
them up, he unfastened his stiff collar and pulled his shirt off over
his head. Some men slept in their shirts, but Will preferred to put
on his long night shirt. He was lucky too in that he wore congress
shoes with elastic sides, which were easy to take off and put on.

"I think it is very unfair, Will. You men have a much easier time of undressing, and besides there is room for four or five men in your washroom at one time."

"Just be thankful that you don't have to shave on a jolting train, darling."

There was no denying that the little berth was snug for two people—not that Janette minded that. It was rather cozy to lie in the dark all shut in, and hear the deep sonorous whistle of the engine and the rhythmic pounding of the wheels as the train sped along through the night. She was more nervous than she dared admit and imagined all sorts of frightening things. But lying beside Will who was so calm and unworried, she put by her fears. Sleep, however, was neither sweet nor refreshing. They would no sooner get to sleep than the train would stop with a jerk that shook the whole car. And when it started again the jerk and jolt were just as bad.

Janette's Diary continues, telling of reaching Pittsburg:

"About midnight we awoke to look out over the city of fire, instead of the city of smoke, as I had always heard it termed. The many furnaces sending out great sheets of light reminded one of the Judgment Day."

When morning came, the ordeal of dressing was even worse than the undressing. Janette had to stand in line with a lot of dishevelled women to await her turn. When she finally did get into the wash room, it was hard to stand upright as the train went around curves. While she was trying to wash, the impatient women who were waiting outside, ready to take her place, kept pounding on the door and twisting the handle. To her this was the most miserable part of the whole trip.

The train having no diner, they stopped at an eating house for breakfast:

"We breakfasted at Cresline, Ohio. The low level land with its small houses and barns, mere stables, all frame was in great contrast to our Pennsylvania buildings. Fields large, fences three rails high, wind pumps numerous.

"Soon we were at Chicago, that busy city but saw little of it. We crossed the Mississippi at Davenport and instead of being impressed with its length and greatness, we saw a shallow clear beautiful stream. 'Twas there I might have lost my pearl ring for I left it in the dressing room and when I missed it, the door was locked and the porter off the car. But I got it again."

II. Westward Ho

As they were crossing the continent, Will wrote lengthy accounts of their trip for the *"Chester Valley Union,"* the most important paper in Chester County, Pennsylvania. Sometimes he signed them, "Traveller," and later "Circumspectus." After the first few days, Janette let him do much of the writing until they reached San Francisco, and later on pasted the clippings into her Diary.

Will starts out with a poem:

> "We'll tread the prairies as of old
> Our fathers sailed the sea,
> And make the West as they the East
> The homestead of the free."

"Tuesday evening, the 19th of June we got in our berth at Chicago, expecting to wake up in Davenport, Iowa, and be in Kansas City on Wednesday evening. The first was realized, the second deferred. After running less than a hundred miles from Davenport, we were told that we would have to get out and wait until the evening train, as the track ahead was not passable on account of the floods. The stopping place was Eldon, on Des Moines River, a lonesome little town of 800 people and a few swine, but the midnight train only brought another load of passengers; the noon train, ditto, and likewise the midnight and noon once more. The little town with its muddy streets, and no streets at all, became alive with strangers and its accommodating resources were well tested. Rain continued to fall at intervals and the water to rise. Telegrams gave but little encouragement, papers were not to be had, so news was scarce."

Janette's Diary adds her account to his:

June 23.

"We were delayed 3 days at Eldon, Iowa, on account of floods, a dismal little town. When we started on Friday afternoon after the bridges and track had been repaired, it seemed like going into a good deal of danger, we were just at supper and as the train sped along with water half way up the car, while we lost our appetites. So long as 'twas light, we eagerly watched the track. All night long we rode through the flooded country. Ere it grew too dark we could see homes deserted, fields of grain flooded and trees and bushes swimming. As it grew darker and darker, and the waters roared around us and the engine steamed bravely on, the conductor and train men wandered up and down the train now talking with passengers now out on the step with a lantern and some tried to sing. My fears increased until I know I must have pictured terrible things. We heard a whistle, and soon met a train and heard all was right ahead. As we neared the Missouri River about 1 A.M., a heavy thunderstorm came up and lasted 20 minutes raging furiously. Our train stopped and there we were for a couple of hours—no one could sleep. The peals of thunder and flashes of lightning were terrible."

When the water was at its highest Janette started to laugh to herself.

"What is so funny, dear?" asked Will. "A penny for your thoughts."

"Oh," laughed Janette, "I was just remembering how you said that you would go as a missionary to Oregon, 'come hell or high water.' Pittsburgh certainly looked like the bad place and now we are assuredly going through 'high water'."

At that Will joined in her laughter: "I am glad that you have some amusing thoughts at this time."

"Well," she replied, "I used to call you stubborn and obstinate."

"What, me stubborn and obstinate?" he asked in surprise.

"Oh, now I know that you are only persevering and determined to reach your goal."

Coming from a long line of Scotch-Irish Presbyterians, Will had to admit that he was determined, to say the least.

"You remember, dear, that sometimes persistence is a good thing. I might not have won you if I hadn't been persistent."

Janette gave him a loving smile. She recalled the time when she felt that because of her cough she and Will should not marry. After days and nights of mental agony, she bolstered up her courage to tell him of her decision. He refused to accept it. He decided at once that he would give up the position that had been offered him in a growing church near home. Instead he asked the Presbyterian Board to send him West as a Home Missionary. He convinced her that out there, in a less severe climate, she could regain her health. Her cough had been so much better in the past year that she felt encouraged, and so they were married as they had planned.

As the rain poured down, the flashes of lightning revealed the crops almost covered by water, and they could hear the water rushing along by the tracks. It was a frightening time. Will quoted from the Psalms: "When thou passest through the waters, I will be with thee and through the rivers, they shall not overflow thee." He started to sing softly, Janette joined in and so did one after another of the passengers:

> "When through the deep waters
> I call thee to go,
> The rivers of sorrow shall not overflow;
> For I will be with thee, thy trouble to bless,
> And sanctify to thee, thy deepest distress."

Then they went on to sing other familiar hymns.

Now to go back to Janette's Diary, June 23:

> "After it was over, we went on to the river's edge and found that the R.R. bridge had been washed away, so we were piloted down a slippery, clayey bank to a vessel and taken across to Kansas City where we went to bed at 4 A.M. asking not to be disturbed. At ten we were awakened by the chambermaid wanting to make the bed. The water was so muddy in the basin, it would not run away. Will sent the pitcher for clean water. Soon the girl returned with more of the same 'coffee,' I called it."

Their stay in Kansas City proved quite pleasant, owing to the kindness of her cousin, John C. Mickle. John had already made the trip West, so he said: "My advice to you is to take along some extra food in your lunch baskets. It will save your temper when there are long waits between meals. You can get sandwiches, hot coffee or tea, biscuit and fruit at the lunch counters if you don't want a regular meal." His wife Martha gave them some home-cooked food for their lunch baskets.

Will's account continued:

> "We determined to take the A.T. and S.F. R.R. having heard so much of its scenic beauty, but it is not necessary to praise the truly grand, though it is indeed praiseworthy. Of the prairies and plains we have no word to speak."

One advantage that they had in taking the Atcheson, Topeka

and Santa Fe Railroad was the Harvey Houses, where the trains usually stopped thirty minutes for meals. Their reputation for food was well known. Fred Harvey did for his eating houses what George Pullman did for the sleeping cars and "Hotel Coaches." When Janette saw the clean tablecloths, napkins, and real silver, she exclaimed: "Why this looks like home!"

Will beckoned to a neatly uniformed girl, who greeted him with a smile and took his order. They exchanged a few remarks about the trip and the weather. After she had left, Janette whispered: "Now, Will, don't you dare flirt with that pretty blond waitress."

"Don't worry," he said with a laugh. "Bye-the-bye, these Harvey girls don't last long since they get so many offers of matrimony."

After dining with Fred Harvey many passengers were unwilling to put up with the eating houses on some other lines, where the food was greasy and poorly cooked and served. They called them such unflattering names as "Swill Pail Route" or "Ptomaine Limited."

At Topeka, Kansas, they were supposed to stop for twenty minutes for lunch. Janette and Will had to wait their turn to order, and were settling down to eat when the bell rang and the whistle blew.

"Why, what is the meaning of this?" Will asked the conductor and pulled out his watch. "It is only a quarter past twelve and we are not due to leave until twelve thirty."

The conductor then showed him his watch that said 12:30 and explained, "That's because we run on 'sun-time.' Each train figures that out. We may be on time by our own time, but late by others. But now a commission is working on the problem. They hope that by next November all railway clocks and watches will be put on to a standard time."

Since they had to pay in advance, there was nothing to do but to pile back onto the train, leaving most of the meal uneaten. They stopped for supper at Abilene [Kansas], where the train waited thirty minutes just opposite the Harvey House. Here they got a very good meal.

At Kit Carson, Colorado, named for the old hunter, trapper and guide, the day being clear, they caught their first view of Pike's Peak and the Rockies. It was specially thrilling to Janette to get her first view of those wonderful mountains. To her this was all new, though not to Will since he had been there in the summer of 1881 when he was still a student of theology. Will drew out a notebook from his vest pocket and read to Janette this flowery description, which he had copied down from the Pacific Tourist, Henry T. Williams, Editor, published in New York in 1880:

"The tourist is full of enthusiasm. It is this keen, beautiful, refreshing, oxygenated, invigorating, toning and enlivening mountain air which is giving him the glow of nature."

They both laughed over the many adjectives, then Janette remarked, as they stood out on the rear platform where there was an abundance of the highly praised mountain air:

"I do believe, Will, that it is beginning to work. I feel much more energetic here."

Stopping off at Pueblo, Colorado, they went up to Manitou to view nature's own art gallery, as seen in the Garden of the Gods. Janette was entranced by the red and yellow walls of sandstone. To her they looked like a theatrical scene. Or as if the Norse gods of Walhalla in an outburst of rage had tossed the jagged rocks of rich terra cotta red, so that they stood tilted against the intense blue of the sky. The ground was also red and covered with a pattern of mosses and grass. Above all was the majestic top of Pike's Peak.

On June 26th they stopped at Colorado Springs, which had been laid out as a health resort ten years before. Twenty thousand trees were planted. Will was pleased to know that there were no saloons or gambling halls, so he thought it was the Garden of Eden. When the maid at the hotel learned that they planned to climb Pike's Peak on horseback, she said to Janette:

"I'm telling you, Miss, if you don't put on plenty of cold cream and powder, your nose is going to be burned to a blister."

Janette thanked her and applied three layers of cold cream and powder until Will laughingly called her a "whited sepulchre." She tied veils on over her head. Then they went out and met the rest of the party, strapped bundles of overcoats and shawls on back of the saddles, and mounted their "bony bronchos," as one of the party called them, for the trip of fourteen miles up and fourteen miles down.

On Wednesday, June 27, Will wrote:

"The party with which we made the ascent had twenty-four in it including guides. A good-sized fat man, of the New York bar, as funny man; an old man of eighty-four, as sage and adviser; two or three men and their wives and several city lads and lasses who became more or less acquainted ere the jaunt was over.

"The road is only a single file one, on one side rises the bluff mountain side, on the other is a deep ravine. Now you follow the trail around a sharp ledge which winds precipitously up among the small underbrush, and from your saddle you can pick some fragrant mountain flowers."

The sky was clear and cool. Near a snow bank they could sit and gather flowers with one hand and snow with the other. Janette was delighted with the many kinds of flowers she saw in a little mountain meadow: larkspurs, asters, sunflowers, pink gillias, purple penstamen flowers, wild roses, verbenas, columbine (Colorado's state flower), marigolds and blue-bells. They passed the timberline at 11,625 feet. Above them was the rose-red summit with streaks and patches of snow bringing out its beautiful colors.

The panting horses toiled along the narrow pathway, and had to stop to breathe often as they got into the higher and rarer air. It was chilly so the riders were glad to stop and put on their coats. They could see the sun on the red sandstone gateways of the Garden of the Gods. The view was almost overwhelming. On one side were the plains that stretched away like the sea until lost in the misty horizon. Here and there were dots of pine forests and winding threads of green that marked the course of the rivers. On the other side rose lofty mountains, peak on peak, until the eye was bewildered.

Will's story continued:

"Soon you are above timberline and crossing the rugged boulder fields. Vegetation of any kind is scarce but as you cast your eye back over the route you have come, through the clear air you see mountain-lakes, snowcapped peaks, belts of mountain timber and villages nestled at the base and in the plain below. The U.S. signal service is on the summit. Snow fell while we were there, and our drinking water was melted snow, which runs down the mountainside here and there in small streams. To get a full appreciation of the effect, each must see for himself. The height may make you breathe hard but you will be glad you are there. You may feel like singing the 'Long meter' [Doxology] but you won't do it, now that you are 14,500 feet above the sea. The ride down, step by step, jolt by jolt, plunge by plunge, is not pleasant to describe

or to recall.   You will be glad to be down and on the ground
again, if your experience is like mine."

Will's account continued the next day, Thursday, June 28:

"Next we went to Denver, marking its thrift and improvement. Thrift for it aims to make itself the center for the
jobbing trade of that part of the West. Beauty for exclusive
of the strictly business area, it is not a city of houses and
stores so much as of comfortable and neat homes with yards
of well selected flowers, and the streets on either side adorned
by rows of trees. Of its great growth there is no need to
speak. From nothing in 1858 to 65,000 in 1880."

They took the Denver and Rio Grande Railway as far as Salt
Lake City. This was a real adventure for them, as the road had
been opened only a few weeks before and it was their first experience
on a narrow-gauge line. This train, nevertheless, carried a diner.
Janette felt that they took their lives in their hands every time they
crossed to it from their car. It was not only the open space on either
side that made it so dangerous, but the swaying of platforms as
the train lurched around the curves. It was the duty of the dining
car steward to help elderly people and women and children across
between the cars. Janette managed, however, by holding tightly to
the hand rails while Will went ahead to open the heavy door.

The dining car's kitchen was small and compact but was able
to serve good meals. Passengers were offered their choice of quail,
partridge, venison and antelope steak. Filet of beef cost two-bits,
and porterhouse steak, seventy-five cents. The only unpleasant part
was the dust and cinders that came in through the open windows.

Will was very much impressed with the Royal Gorge of the
Arkansas, and wrote:

"Of all the deep canyons penetrated by railways, this is
the most celebrated. As the river bluffs suddenly narrow, the
train plunges with a roar into the Royal Gorge. The railroad
track is ten to twelve feet above the river, close against the
opposite wall. The rocks are many-hued and covered with
moss, and the canyons are so crooked that they seem to close
up before and behind and imprison the train in the narrow
space. Suddenly the walls shut together, 'till one can almost
touch them on either side from the view car and the river runs
through a cleft only thirty feet wide, its granite banks rising
3000 feet on either side. In this grandeur of the Royal Gorge

the traveller is awed into reverent silence. All the while you are getting higher up the mountain and through Marshall Pass. The highest point is 11,730 feet, and the railroad track up the side is not unlike the trail of a snake.

"We were told before starting, that in case anything broke, the automatic air brake would prevent an accident. This we had the pleasure of seing demonstrated when a coupler broke and left us standing still, while our two engines went on. In a number of places you can look back and see the track over which you have come in three or four different places.

"We next came to the Black Canyon of the Gunnison, which is more rugged though not so high with more diversity of scenery than that of the Arkansas. Here a solid wall, there a detachment of rocks standing out like a sentinel; here a curiously formed rock with a stream of water pouring out of its side and dashing to the rapid stream below. On we pass through it and up a tedious ride across a part of the Great American Desert, we stop and admire Castle Gate Rock, and slake our thirst at its base, and then proceed on our desert ride until we emerge into the Utah Valley, a very rich and productive valley settled mostly by Mormons."

At Springville and again at Provo, in Utah, Janette's and Will's train was met by two or three little girls, who held up to the windows baskets of fruit—apples, pears and raspberries. They offered handfuls of fruit for five cents. Janette was charmed by their sweet manner of offering their wares, and bought some from each. Soon they came to Salt Lake City where, as Will put it, they were "looking at a new and strange sort of civilisation . . . where a multitude of new and strange sights met our gaze."

III. From the Mountains to the Sea

Will gives his description of Salt Lake City, which they reached on Sunday, July 1:

"We entered the rich Utah Valley, which lies nestled among the mountains. The soil is said to be eight to ten feet thick in places. It certainly yields good crops and shows the success of irrigation. The settlement is almost exclusively of Mormons. The Mormon Mecca—Salt Lake City—has very long blocks and broad streets, which at this season of the year are very dusty. We went to the Tithing House which is their largest one, and is a depository for the freewill offerings of the people. The tithes are paid in whatever produce they care to bring.

"But a more interesting thing is the Tabernacle service, which we attended on Sunday at two o'clock. The Tabernacle is an elliptical shaped building, with an immense seating capacity, and nearly perfect acoustic properties."

They enjoyed the famous organ and choir but were not greatly impressed with the sermon. "The speaker," Will wrote, "took no text—only spoke as the spirit moved him, whence the spirit we do not dare suggest." They visited the unfinished temple, begun thirty years before.

At Salt Lake City they transferred to the Central Pacific Railroad. Soon after leaving Ogden they had a fine view of the Great Salt Lake. On this line they found most of the eating houses very good being plentifully supplied with meat, fish, game and fruits. Sometimes Will got coffee in a little covered pail that Janette could heat on a flat-topped stove at the end of the car, but he preferred milk when he could get it. Here they saw their first "heathen Chinee," as the Chinese did all the cooking and waiting on tables. They wore short white linen coats over baggy black pants, and their pig-tails were tightly wound about their heads. They hurried here and there, tending to the needs of the customers. Having helped raise money to send to the missionaries in China, Janette was interested in seeing these aliens from that far land. She wondered if they felt the same longing for their home that she did for hers.

The ride across the "Great American Desert" was tedious. There was nothing but sagebrush, rocks and sand. Will fidgeted around and finally got out a book to read, while Janette worked on her Diary. His book, "Two Years in Oregon," by Wallis Nash, was one that he had bought when he learned that he might be sent to Oregon. On the inside of the cover he had pasted his bookplate: "Library of W. S. Young. No. 510. March 3, 1883." (At the age of 23 he had already accumulated over 500 books). That book was published in New York in 1881. Mr. Nash was an Englishman. He said it was "A guide book for the intending emigrant, but others may be interested in the picture of a young community shaping the details of their common life and claiming and taking possession of a heritage in the wilderness."

When Will came to something amusing or especially interesting he read it aloud to Janette. "Listen to this," he said with a chuckle:

"A law was passed giving a half section of land to every settler and half another to his wife. Often a man accompanied by a Justice of the Peace would ride up to a cabin door on his cayuse and call out, 'Is there a likely gal here?' And often a thirteen or fourteen old girl would be married then and there to a man old enough to be her father.

"I heard of one Justice of the Peace known for his expeditious ways, before whose house a runaway couple halted in their wagon. The man shouted for the Justice who appeared.

'Say, Judge, can you marry us right away?'

'I guess so, my son,' he replied.

'Well, then let's have it.'

"Whereupon the Justice mounted the wagon-wheel and there stood with his foot upon the hub.

'What's your name?' he asked.

'Jehosophat Smith.'

'Well, then, wilt thou have this woman, so help you God?'

'Yes.'

'My fee's a dollar; drive on'."

Janette joined in his laughter. "At that rate, Will, your marriage fees won't be very high, and you know they always go to the minister's wife."

Janette and Will had read a great deal about the early history of the Presbyterian Church in Oregon Territory, where the first Presbyterian Church west of the Rockies was founded August 18,

1838.   Will had been interested to learn that one of the eight children of Elkanah and Mary Walker, early pioneer missionaries, was named for Levi Chamberlain, a missionary in Honolulu whose wife was Will's aunt, Maria Patton.   The Chamberlains went to Honolulu on a whaling ship about 1820, and Chamberlain became "Superintendent of Secular Affairs, Sandwich Islands Mission."

Among Janette's treasured keepsakes was an album presented to her by her pupils of the Spring Grove School, at Christmas, 1882. During the long ride across the desert she got it out of her satchel and reread some of the messages to gain comfort.   Shortly before they left Parkesburg her father had written in the album in his fine Spencerian handwriting, dated June 13:

"To Jennie:
There is another album
Full of leaves of snowy white;
Where no name is ever tarnished
But forever pure and bright
In the Book of Life, - God's Album,
May your name he penned with care
And may all who here have written
Write their names fovever there.
            Lovingly,
            Your Father."

Sister Annie wrote:
"May your life be one of happiness and peace," then added a footnote,
"Who will break in your shoes now?"
Her friend Sue wrote:
"Now that you are married
A broom to you I'll send
In sunshine use the brushy part
In storm the other end."
Sallie Boyd had written:
"As you follow the setting sun, let its beautiful light rest upon your heart and keep it ever as your name 'Young'."
Their lawyer Cousin Arthur Parke wrote:
"Fee simple and a simple fee
And all the fees in tail
Are nothing when compared to thee
Thou best of fees — fe-male."

Brother Thomas Young wrote:

"May you spend happy days in Oregon and return home again safe."

Her grandma Sarah Lewis wrote:

"You will find my very
Best wishes for you in the
Last four verses of the sixth
Chapter of Numbers."

Janette got out her Bible and read over again those precious words, and it seemed as if dear Grandma was speaking to her.

It was stifling hot in the car, and when they opened the windows the cinders came in until Janette's dainty hemstiched white collar and cuffs and Will's shirt were streaked with dirt. Janette got a cinder in her eye and under pretext of removing it had a chance to shed a few tears as a wave of homesickness engulfed her. She had heard of a God-forsaken country, and this it must surely be.

When Will saw how uncomfortable Janette was he said contritely, "Darling, I am sorry that we couldn't have taken the Hotel Car train. They have a fine dining car and Silver Palace sleeping cars. If we were on that you could play on the melodeon or a Burdette organ with all the stops and pedals. But," he added ruefully, "it would have cost ten dollars more."

Janette managed to smile: "Now, Will dear, don't worry about me. That is a luxury that we can forego. Since the Presbyterian Board is paying our fare, we could hardly ask for that very expensive train with all its fancy mahogany woodwork, elaborate decorations and special menus served in the dining car."

Frequently in those days there were train wrecks. With wooden cars, even when they had steel frames, the fire from the lighted candles or kerosene lamps often made the accidents much worse. They passed a bad wreck not far from Wells, Nevada, and took on board some of the injured passengers. It had happened only a short time before. A newspaper clipping, pasted in the Diary describes it:

"The engine was completely wrecked and the two cars thrown from the track and pretty badly mashed up. The emigrant car filled with women and children, was turned upside down, and the poor, screaming and wailing mass had to be taken out of the windows of the car."

At Wells, a regular stop, the green meadows were a refreshing sight. Here in early times the emigrants used to camp to rest their teams after their long hard journey across the desert. But now the emigrant trains marked the end of the ox-team era. Occasionally they would pass one of these trains standing on a siding, for they were often side-tracked. They were mixed trains, part freight and part passenger. They lacked some of the refinements found elsewhere—thus the seats were made of slats. The people carried their own bedding and their food, which they cooked or heated on a flat-topped stove. The men were rough looking, and some of the women looked foreign with shawls over their heads. Little children waved from the windows. All, however, seemed to be having a good time and shared each other's food just as they did in the covered wagon days.

They also saw "Zulu" cars. When families took their horses or cows west with them, one member of the family could ride free. They always had more milk than they could use, since the cows had to be milked night and morning. Many families engaged a whole freight car and brought with them all their household goods, furniture, farm machinery, buggies and wagons.

At Elko, Nevada, they stopped for supper and had an excellent meal in a neat well-kept dining room. It was in the midst of a game and fish country, so they dined well. They were interested in seeing the Indians, mostly Shoshones, who gathered around the station to beg from the passengers. By paying two-bits to one of the squaws, they removed a piece of dirty cloth so that they could see the face of a little papoose who stared at them with his beady eyes.

For breakfast they stopped at the desert station of Humdoldt, Nevada. In spite of the bare appearance they found the dining room neat and clean. They learned that it was famous for its good meals. They also enjoyed the clear cold spring water. Their train was held up by a hot-box, so they walked about in the shade of the cottonwoods. Janette thought with pity of the slatternly-dressed women, the wives of the railroad workers, who lived in houses built of railroad ties.

As they journeyed farther west, Janette wrote in her Diary:
"At noon when the train stopped for dinner, we were told that the train ahead had eaten everything, so, on we went. Soon came to a wreck. A small culvert had been burned leaving the track in place and the engineer did not see any danger until the engine went down. Engine, baggage car and two or three other cars were ruined—no one injured."

They were glad when the scenery changed and they entered a mountain canyon, with pines, incense cedars and fir trees on the slopes and the Truckee river down below. They resented the endless snow-sheds that cut off their view. It was tantalizing to be boxed up when in the midst of such glorious scenery. After passing through one snowshed, twenty-eight miles long, the train emerged into the sunlight. The view of the hills and the distant mountains covered with tall pines was worth waiting for. Down below them they caught glimpses of Donner Lake, lying like a jewel in its woodland setting. They recalled the stories that they had heard of the Donner party, who were caught there by the heavy snows in the winter of 1846-47. Of the 90 people in the party, 42 had died before a rescue party could reach them. They passed Emigrant Gap, where the emigrants let their wagons down the steep mountain side by ropes, with which a turn or two was taken about trees.

As the train approached Colfax, California, the conductor told them that not long ago there had been a race between the train and a large herd of deer. When the train entered the narrow valley, a large herd of red deer were surprised as they were drinking at a spring. The engineer blew his whistle, which so frightened them that they dashed down the road ahead of the train. The engineer put on steam and they kept ahead for seven miles. Finally when they came to more open country, they ran to one side and looked at the train in amazement as it rushed past.

From Colfax they passed lumber towns with piles of Douglas fir logs, stacks of fresh planking and piles of bright yellow sawdust. Then on past mining towns with their heaps of water-washed gravel. Flumes made of timber ran for miles.

The train stopped for a meal at Sacramento. Then at Benicia their train crossed the great river on the "Solano," the largest ferryboat in the world. It carried four lines of track. They had thirty miles of splendid views before they came to Oakland, and to a pier two and a half miles long, large enough to accommodate steamships that came from China, the Sandwich Islands, Australia and Alaska. It had a double line of rails its whole length.

At the station they found the ferryboat to cross the Bay. Passengers and baggage were quickly moved into this magnificent boat. On July 3, they reached the landing stage of the most westerly big city of the American Continent, San Francisco. Here were waiting omnibuses from all the main hotels. Theirs was the Palace Hotel, which they thought was almost a town in itself. It covered three acres and could accommodate 1200 guests.

There were then no through trains to Oregon. The Northern Pacific was building westward from Bismarck, Dakota, and at the same time eastward from Portland. And the Southern Pacific was working on a link between Sacramento and Portland. They could have gone part way on this by rail, and the rest of the way by stage, taking six days. But they preferred to go by sea.

Since their ship would not leave for two days, they had time for sight-seeing. The cool weather was very welcome after the heat of the desert. They found that San Francisco, like Rome, was built on seven hills. They soon learned that they must never say, "Frisco." Their room gave them a fine view of the city, rising picturesquely from the water. The houses were of wood, and many had handsome carvings around the doors and windows. Bow windows were very popular, and in most were flowering plants and bird cages. From these windows the occupants could watch the passers-by, and still avoid the cold winds from off the Pacific.

They wanted to ride on the cable cars after hearing so much about them. So they boarded one, painted a dirty mustard yellow, to go up California Street. The steep hills terrified Janette. She hung on tightly as the car lurched and rushed up one hill and down another. When passengers wished to get off or others wanted to get on, the motorman clanged his bell and the car jerked to a stop. The conductor was very polite in helping ladies with bundles and small children. He called to a hurrying woman who was waving frantically, "Take your time, Madame." Janette said, "They wouldn't say that in New York."

They had heard of the "Big Four," and the scandal of the land grants connected with the building of the railroads. So they were interested when the conductor pointed out the mansions of Collis P. Huntington, Leland Stanford, Mark Hopkins, and Charles Crocker on Nob Hill - "snob hill," he called it. Leland Stanford was no longer living in his big mansion, but had built another on a 9,000 acre ranch down the coast in Palo Alto. There he kept hundreds of blooded horses and had two race tracks. "Not a God-fearing man," was Will's conclusion.

From the top of Nob Hill they had a breath-taking view of all of San Francisco and the harbor, crowded with ships of many nations.   Across the bay eastward were Oakland, Berkeley, and Ala-meda, and Mt. Tamalpais in the distance to the north.

On their way back, Will said, "Let's get off and see China-town." They walked through the narrow cobble-stoned streets.   The buildings were two or three stories high.   In the many small shops they saw fine china, jade, carved ivory, brocades and other treasures from the Far East.   From the many balconies hung huge signs carved and painted in red and gold.   The peaked roofs with upturned eaves looked strange.   Over them floated the dragon flag of China.   The streets were squalid and dirty.   There were smells that even the burning incense could not deaden, so that they were obliged to hold their noses at times.   They had heard tales of slave girls and opium dens.   Janette was glad to learn that the Presbyterians had the oldest and largest mission for work among the Chinese in San Francisco, and were active in rescuing the slave girls.

They wished that they could have been there for the Chinese New Year, celebrated in February.   Then, they were told, all of Chinatown was gay and festive with lighted lanterns and embroi-dered banners.   The Chinese ladies would appear on the streets, exquisitely dressed in silks and brocades, tottering along on their bound "lily feet."   The servant girls were the lucky ones, as their feet were not bound.   The little Chinese children in their bright-colored dresses were like gay butterflies.   Along the street on narrow shelves were displayed Chinese lily blooms, mandarin oranges, cakes sprinkled with sesame seeds, almond cakes, sugared cocoanut, candied melon rind, ginger and dried lechee nuts.   The hundred-footed dragon wound its way through the street, to the sounds of the ex-ploding firecrackers.   All the Chinese living in California, who pos-sibly could, gathered there for the celebration.

They visited the Cliff House and dined at the restaurant at the edge of the cliffs, facing west.   They heard the roar of the waves breaking against Seal Rocks, where the seals basked in the sunshine or swam in the surf.   Their harsh barking sounded above the noise of the breakers.   They decided that San Francisco was a wonderful place to visit.

IV. *So this is Oregon*

Janette and Will left San Francisco on the Steamer *Queen of the Pacific* on Thursday, July 3, at 10 A.M. They were delighted at the thought of a sea voyage. Neither had ever been on a ship before. They stowed their luggage in the neat little cabin, and went up on deck for a view of San Francisco Harbor, lying protected by the hills. There was a motley lot of ships in the port, which added to their interest as they tried to identify the various flags flying at the masts. Even the people looked strange to them. There were rough miners, in their heavy boots and flannel shirts, who had made money in the gold mines and were on their way back to Oregon. There were sunburned farmers in rough clothes as well as some flashily dressed men who were already trying to get some of the miners into a card game.

Janette was surprised to see a number of women on board. She thought their clothes were much too fancy for such a trip. She had put aside her grey silk travelling dress for something more practical soon after starting their journey. They said that they were going to Alaska, but only laughed a great deal when she asked if their husbands were up there.

Down below on the steerage deck she saw a number of queer-looking Chinamen with long pigtails. She could hear them jabbering in their peculiar language. Will said that he had heard that they were going up to work for the Oregon Railway and Navigation Company.

"In Oregon," he added, "you will see many Chinese signs hanging in the streets such as 'Hop Kee,' 'Sam Lin,' 'Lee Chung' or 'Ah Sin,' as they do all the laundry"

The call came, "All ashore that's going ashore," and soon the ship got under way. As they stood on deck they were thrilled at the beauty of the Golden Gate. It was rightly named, they felt.

After they left the protection of the Bay, the water became rough and the ship began to roll. Janette found that she wasn't as good a sailor as she had thought. She wrote in her Diary, July 5:

"Left San Francisco on Steamer 'Queen of the Pacific' on Thurs. at 10 A.M. The hurry and worry of attending to

baggage so tired Will that he attributed what little squeamish-
ness he had to that instead of frankly owning that old ocean
caused it.   How he ran around, how he laughed, talked and
read as after taking the first meal I laid me down in my neat
white berth, there to remain for the whole trip.   While memory
lasts a vivid recollection of the trip shall remain with me.   Will
read Handy Andy to me but had to laugh for both of us, he
did not miss a single meal, took a savage delight in telling me
how very few were at the table and how he enjoyed the rich
dinners.   The dozen lemons were not used.   The little tin con-
tribution box hung constantly at my side wide open, waiting.
The vessel had two motions, one like a rocking chair, the other
like a cradle, we had a room in the center of the vessel close
to the engine room, as one and another of the ladies got able
to go on deck, they could look in and see me lying pale and
listless in my berth and inquired kindly for me.   But sea-sick-
ness like all else has an end but it is not all attributed to
imagination for Mr. Hill affirms that a deer they had on board
from Alaska died from it.   Mrs. Canthorn (Gervais) says if ever
she writes a book her hero and heroine shall not take their
wedding trip to Europe!

"But on reaching the Columbia river our spirits revived
and we stepped ashore at Astoria, Or.   I was still so weak I
could scarcely drag along.   Writing poetry is not my forte,
nevertheless when one's inner depths are stirred as if by a
churn dasher, the mind takes new and strange freaks, it led me
to send this back to Penna.

'Here lies your old friend Mrs. Y.
Seasick and homesick and ready to die
Yet if the message should come just now
A faint low 'No' would be given I vow.
If ever you marry, leave such a trip late
For a seasick woman is a cranky old mate'."

When Janette was feeling very wretched she said, "Oh Will,
dear, I wish now that instead of coming by ship, we had taken the
Central Pacific Railroad to Redding, then the stage to Roseburg,
where we could take the Oregon California Railway to Portland."
"Yes, that would have been fine and the scenery they say is
beautiful along the Sacramento River and past Mt. Shasta.   But that
would have taken six days, and I thought you didn't want that 275

mile ride over rough roads in the stage. And remember, hold-ups are common on those mountain roads."

"Well," she replied "that was before I knew that I would be seasick."

As they reached the Columbia River, Janette was once more her gay and happy self. She thought the town of Astoria was not very attractive. It had a fine location at the mouth of the river, but the main part of the town was built on piles and there were many fish canneries and lumber mills. The people lived in little white houses scattered among the fir-tree covered hills. Here was built one of the oldest Presbyterian Churches for white people on the Pacific coast.

As the ship went up the hundred miles to Portland, they saw the steep rocky banks rising on either side of the river. Above, the slopes were covered with a dense growth of fir, spruce and hemlock trees. They saw more lumber mills, fish canneries and some small farms. In the distance they saw higher hills but alas, the gorgeous snow-capped peaks of Mt. Hood, Mt. Adams, and Mt. Saint Helen were covered by clouds.

As they neared Portland Will remarked: "It is hard to believe that there were only a few log huts here 35 years ago and that now it is a city of about 20,000."

Janette wrote:

July 7.

"We landed at Portland at 8:30 P.M. and ... were welcomed as if old friends. On Sunday we attended Calvary Church. Mr. Lee, the Pastor and a Seminary mate of Will's soon recognized him and invited him into the pulpit to assist. In the evening we went to the new Market Theater where Mr. Lee was holding gospel meetings for the masses.

"Portland is a business place though with many fine residences but it was dusty and smoky and we were not much pleased with it."

July 9.

"After spending a pleasant Sabbath we left Mon. for Woodburn. The valley looked strange to us. In the cars we met again a lady who had been traveling with us in the vessel, Mrs. E.N. Cook. From her we learned an attempt had been made on the life of Senator Voorhees a few weeks before. It was to his home we were directed to go by Rev. R.W. Hill.

We learned however he had recovered. Getting off the train no one greeted us we having failed to notify Mr. V. Will inquired where he lived and then leaving me to wait in the ticket office, off he started with Mr. Proctor to walk a mile and a half. As they went out the door they both stopped, drew out their watches to compare time with the little clock in the office. Mr. Proctor, 'Why is that time correct?' Will, 'I'm twenty minutes slow according to it and I've Portland time.' Nevertheless Mr. P. set his watch by it and away they went and I was left to pass the time as best I could in the little western village. I read all that was interesting in a newspaper lying there. I wished that the operator would come in that I might ask permission to use his pen and ink but the presence of a lady in his apartments was so novel to him that he only ventured in long enough to take a message and then out again to sit and talk with the men outside. If ever I make his acquaintance it will be a relief to me to assure him I had no intention of playing cannibal. Finally I took out pencil and paper and took down my impressions of what I looked upon as my future home.

"People looked strange. I wondered what thoughts occupied their minds, what feelings actuated them, houses looked strange. I wondered if the outside was indicative of the inside, the forest of fir trees that skirted the place looked strange and dark and I wondered if it ever hid secrets. But my reverie was broken by the return of that husband of mine with a two horse wagon. Loading us in baggage and all, off we drove through heat and dust two miles out in the country. Will had gotten the mail that was awaiting us and as we jolted along we read letters from the dear home folks that we had left just three weeks before and from whom we had not heard except from Annie in Denver. Oh, how homesick it made me, how I longed to see them, how it all rushed over me that they gave their consent unwillingly to have us come so far and how it was possible I might never see them. But not alone for Will's sake I restrained my tears but because of the cloud of dust that enveloped us . . .

"Mrs. Vorhees a genial little woman met us at the gate and welcomed us to their home, such a whole hearted reception as did us strangers in a strange land good. After a wash, we began to devour the mail that had accumulated, letters came first, the home ones first of all then the others in order . . .

"This done we were ready to be sociable. The family consists of Mr. and Mrs. V. Mollie C. Newton, May and Harry . . . The place is a ranch of 496 acres of which 140 are in wheat, 78 in oats. Fruit plenty though this is a bad season. Meals that of good old-fashioned farmers."

In the evening the Senator told them of the great Willamette Valley to which they had come, which he felt was one of the most favored spots on earth. Already they were favorably impressed with what they saw of Oregon. They liked its greenness and varied landscape, with hills in the north, broad prairies along the Willamette River, and the distant mountains, the Cascades and the Coast Range, on either side. The fields of grain and orchards of fruit trees were separated from the road by "snake" fences made of logs. Along the roadside was a tangle of wild roses, wax berries and wild flowers. The ferns or bracken, so beautiful in the woods, were a pest to the farmer and had to be dug out. It was hard to get used to seeing the blackened stumps in the fields. The farms were not kept up as neatly and did not look as thrifty as those in Pennsylvania. Much of the land was covered with forests. The flower that most appealed to them was the Lilium Washingtonium, a spotted lily that grew in the midst of the wheat fields, scenting all the air with its sweetness.

The Diary of July 9 continues:

"When we left Portland we told them to expect us back by Wednesday to buy furniture but alas we were compelled to learn 'Man proposes, God disposes.' We learned Rev. Mr. Hill had gone to Alaska and left word that Will should preach at Turner till he returned. This was news to Will, who soon saw that this meant two fields instead of one . . . Having spent the week in replying to our kind eastern friends we went to Turner Sat. morning, were met by Mr. and Mrs. S. Condit. Mrs. said she was glad to see the minister bring his wife along, for that looked as if he had come to stay. We rode five miles out in the country to their home where they are comfortably fixed. We spent a quiet afternoon with not very edifying conversation among other things we learned that the ladies hearing of the new minister, had passed opinions about his supposed looks and decided that he would at least have blue eyes. They did not think of him having a wife or they would have had her diagnosed. This is maybe the current matter of the peoples' thoughts?! Evening came and after worship we went to our cage, as Will called it — a wee room off the parlor — 7½ × 8 ft. It contained a bed, two chairs and a washstand. Our first query was how were two persons to undress in such a small space. We managed though by my getting on the bed and as I took off each garment Will found a place to put it. My clothes on the foot of the bed my shoes under the bed, my corsets on the hinge of the door, and at last thrust his pen-knife in the door and hung my ear-rings on it. All the while I sat on the bed holding my sides and making strenuous efforts to smother the laughter that we so feared would be heard through the board partitions."

On July 15 Janette wrote:

"On Sun. morning we locked the house and all went to church. S.S. was held before service. Mr. Condit is Supt. I went in Bible class and we had question and answer! Will made an address."

The church where they held that service had been founded in 1855. Its one-room frame building, Janette wrote, was "the oldest Presbyterian church now standing" in Oregon. That building still stands (see the picture opposite page 48). Mr. Condit told them how he and his brothers had helped their father, the Reverend Philip Condit, build it in 1858. Although all lived in log cabins, they had hauled sawed lumber from Oregon City in order that the Lord's house could be better than their own.

The Diary continues:

"There was an audience of 63, gave good attention. Mrs. Condit led the singing, they have no organ. After service Will went around among the folks making himself acquainted. I waited for introductions and felt just like what I was, the minister's new wife or the new minister's wife or—anybody, but myself! One lady took me for Miss Carey and began questioning me about my return. With two or three I tried to converse but with little success, people seemed glad to see each other but knew not how to welcome a stranger. We returned to Mr. C's, remained over night were brought over to Turner about nine o'clock the next morning to wait for the one o'clock mail. Were taken to Mr. Shaw—but as all were away except the daughter who was in the midst of washing and who gave us no encouragement to remain we left and were driven round to Mr. McKinney's only to find Mrs. K. in like situation. She accepted us though not with open arms and left us to entertain ourselves which was perfectly right considering our forced intrusion, while she went on with her work. Mr. K. came home at noon and we had dinner and as a consequence of the good meal, left for the train with the feeling we had been kindly treated. But these experiences together with an undefinable something which I hope time, and association with the people will clear away, made me feel an unwillingness to go back to Turner. And while long ago I had told myself I would be willing to go with Will wherever he went, when I found that Mr. Hill considered it best that we settle there, something within me revolted and I went away to pray not only that we might be guided to the place where we could both do our best work but that my personal feelings in regard to the Turner field might be overcome."

Senator Vorhees told them of the mix-up of names of Turner and Marion. The railroad had wanted a station at the present site of Turner, near Mill Creek, to be called Marion after Francis Marion of Revolutionary War fame. But by mistake the lumber for the station was put off the train at the present site of Marion. So it was decided to go ahead with the building and call it Marion. Other material was sent to the first place, and the station was named Turner after a near-by farmer.

The Diary of July 15 continues:

"Mrs. Voorhees wanted a girl Mr. V. rode thirty three miles to hunt one, found one who was habitually tired. After being here a few days, she said Mr. V. might have known by the looks of her she could not do the work. Besides she came more for company for the women in their loneliness, than to work!

"At this P.O. when the mail comes in they call the letters off and most people are there to get them. Will was unable to get one or two cent postage stamps or more than half a pack of postals at a time. The new ministers wife was presented with a dozen cups of jelly by Mrs. Rice."

July 22.

"Mr. Voorhees whole family and ourselves to Woodburn to church. The S.S. which was held first was in good working order, from the child of four to the man of seventy five all seemed interested. Twelve years ago there were many spiritualists and infidels the sabbath was not kept and all meetings or conventions ended with dancing. Many were held on Saturday night and ended on Sun. morning.

"But some few Christians as leader Mr. Voorhees, resolved to start an S.S. While parents took no interest themselves but went on with week day work they were willing to let their children attend. At first it was held in a blacksmith shop for which they paid three dollars per month but they saved money by holding it during the summer in a grove. But even the discomfiture of that worked good many persons who would not enter the shop would come and stand around among the trees and look on and in time became interested themselves. Today Woodburn has a neat church and is a temperance village. The saloon keeper complains he is not treated decently!

"The sermon to which we listened was by Mr. Keen a Cumberland Pres. His text Heb. 11, 13-26. A very common expository sermon when persecuted in one verse he fled to the next. Will made closing prayer. In afternoon Will rode to Gervais 4 mi. distant, preached to a congregation of 73 attentive listeners. Mrs. Cauthorne said first sermon by Pres. she had heard in a year. It is a place of 400 inhabitants fully one half of whom are Roman Catholics. They have built a church and convent. The other church built by Baptists is open to all Prot. denominations. On Monday after his eight miles of horseback riding Will thought standing was preferable to sitting.

July 22.

"Will and I rode to Butterville, 8 mi. distant. The sabbath previous a man came down to Mr. V's S.S. and asked him to come up there and start one for them. He was not himself a Christian, he asked it for the benefit of his children. Two a day is all one man can manage and there is no one as yet to send. But Will's idea was to do the next best thing, go and preach, once at least, so we went to make acquaintances and get the people interested. Someone remarked if it were a circus there would be no trouble in getting them to attend. There has been no regular service since 1863 and no preaching at all for three years. People are actually leaving, assigning as their reason they could not risk bringing up their children in such a place . . .

"We returned to B. and called on Mrs. Galland whose husband fell dead in the streets of Portland a short time since. She lived in what looked to be an old ware-house or well, it reminded me of just such a home as Dickens describes. Dingy walls, old paper, old matting, old cracked piano, plenty of books and papers though. Mrs. G. is a well-educated lively little Jewess, passionately fond of music. I played and sang Juanita. Had an invitation to come back and stay as long as I wanted with her and when I returned to my husband she said he would appreciate me more. I should not want it to take long to win his appreciation if I were obliged to stay there! She as well as Mrs. Yergens asked if I had any little boys? We met Mr. and Mrs. Stevens an old couple formerly of N.Y. State who testified to the healthfulness of this climate. In the meantime Will called on Mr. Hobach and found in him a true blue Presbyterian. Having obtained a promise to have news of service circulated freely we took our departure from what seemed a very Sodom for how could God's blessing rest on such a wicked place.

"After a dusty ride we returned to Mr. Voorhees having for me ended an eventful day, my first day of real mission work."

While they were at Woodburn they took time to figure their expenses. Janette, as Will's secretary, copied his letter of July 24, 1883, to Mr. O. D. Eaton of the Presbyterian Board in New York City. In it Will said:

"We are very well pleased with things thus far, are going to have what we came for (viz. work) and that in such proportions that it has only one discouraging feature—so much to be done and so few to do it.

"I enclose the bill of expenses.

Car fares	Phila to Chicago	$ 36.50
	Ch. to K.C.	15.30
	K.C. to San Franc.	120.00
	S.F. to Portland	35.00
	Portland to Woodburn	3.20
		$210.00

Pullman	Phila to Chic.	$ 5.50
	Ch. to Davenport	2.00
	K.C. to Pueblo	5.00
	Pueblo to Ogden	5.00
	Ogden to S.F.	6.00
		$ 23.50
Freight		
	N.Y. to S.F.	53.70
	Phila to S.F.	42.48
	K.C. to S.F.	7.28
On all from S.F. to Woodburn		10.00
		$113.46

Drayage on freight and trunks in
N.Y. Phila. Chicago, K.C., S.F.
and Portland $ 9.60
Meals along the way   16.65

"On account of floods in Iowa, Sunday intervening and waiting for boat at Frisco, hotel bills were incurred to the extent of $18.00."

The total cost of their trip was $391.21.

Of a service at Butterville she wrote on July 30:

"We anticipated opposition yesterday but had an audience of 35. Will had excellent attention, we were told there were even some spiritualists present. He preached from the text, 'I am the way' and it seemed a strange coincidence that behind him on the wall hung the whole verse. Immediately after the sermon we sang, Where is my boy, tonight? with marked effect—it seemed to touch their hearts, one lady wanted me to come to her house and play it again before leaving. In the afternoon Will preached at Whitney's schoolhouse to an audience of 100, 25 of whom were outside waiting, Will said to see how the insiders stood the preaching. I don't know what kind of a wild animal the boys imagined him to be for they watched him open mouthed.

"Three little boys sat on a bench behind him, one picking splinters out of the sole of his foot. When that was done he was ready to take his revenge on the boy at his side who all the while was annoying him. Quick as a wink he turned and punched him. Our attention was divided between Will's firstly and the actions of the little pugilists. Presently a big man with heavy boots walked forward grabbed boy No. 1 and dragged him back, then another bigger man with heavier boots, walked the whole length of the room, grabbed boy No. 2 and marched him back. Boy No. 3 had no alternative but the black-board. During prayer one baby kept calling Mama! Mama!, during sermon girls read papers and books, children ran across the room back and forth but notwithstanding all this the older ones gave good attention, they are anxious to hear the gospel. The people, babies and all had been there since one o'clock. The reason is an old shaggy-bearded gray-headed, bandy legged man called Father Jackson a genuine old time singing master has a singing school from 1 to 3 Mr. V. a S. S. from 3 to 4 and Will had the grande finale 4 to 5. Temperance Societies, picnics and singing schools are held on Sunday. We must not be too severe for the time might be spent more unprofitably. Will goes through his part as if used to it for years. He has resolved to preach but twice a day.

"On the way to church we saw a washing out, met a man with bags of grain, met four men taking header-bed home. Storekeepers do most of their business on Sunday at Gervais . . .

"Mrs. E. [Estey] said to her certain knowledge there had been no service at Butterville for three years. Mrs. Galland had told the other ladies we were to come home with her to dinner, and so stating the same to me she bustled off. After arranging for the S.S. we went to the house and in a few minutes were invited out to an 'impromptu dinner!' The menu included fried salmon which looked good but of the taste I forbear to speak. Bread, which at home would have been fed to the dogs. The butter looked as though taken from around churn handle, oh, how glad Will was he never ate the article and the coffee well two or three mouthfuls made me feel I had not lost all bile yet by the sea voyage. Two or three sips were enough. The plates were of three kinds and sizes. The 'silver spoons' were black tin. The butter knife an old rusty case knife. The stewed apples were quite good the blackberries we did not sample. As Will was fortunate in not drinking coffee he had a cup of milk, judging from the strength of it, the cows had likely been fed on rails. One small bowl of custard was dessert for six. The table was 4 by 2. As W. took no coffee there was a clean saucer for his dessert, we used our coffee saucers. So much for the impromptu dinner with a long ride as sauce to help it down. We swallowed it with pleased faces talking *suavely* all the while of Plutarch and funerals. We have resolved to accommodate ourselves to circumstances, making ourselves easy whether we incline to or not. I wondered though how Will could preach on such diet."

July 31.

"Annie's birthday, think much about her."

August 2.

"We went to Gervais on an errand for Mr. V. and also called on Mrs. Cauthorne. A very pleasant woman—formerly a school teacher. While we were absent R. W. Hill came. After consideration of the work and fields it was decided we live at Turner and endeavor to hold both fields, that is here and there. He gave choice of Silverton or Gervais. Will took latter. It seems impracticable to locate here since most of the work will be up there. This field is hardly ready to be possessed by Presbys. yet, that is already possessed and should be held. The fact is there is work enough in either field for one man, but there is only Will to go to work. The Oregonian states that the Prot. pulpit in Gervais needs a power behind it. An item from Butterville says, 'Rev. Young preached last Sunday for us. We enjoyed a treat'."

The Diary continues:

August 3.

"On the third invitation from Salem. We went Thursday evening. Mr. Crawford met us with a carriage at the train and after our welcome and tea we went to prayer meeting. Will was called on to make a prayer ... In the morning Emma took us around the town. We went all through the new State House. The Governor and most of the Secretaries were out of town, but we met the State Superintendent of Schools and the Librarian. The Senate Chamber had a handsome brussels carpet, we asked why covered with floor linen, were told it was used sometimes for balls."

The State Capitol was on elevated ground, about a mile back from the river. The large lawn in front was artistically planted with trees, shrubs, and flowers. Salem was founded by Methodist missionaries in 1840. The streets were wide and the lots large. There were well-kept gardens full of bright summer flowers and locust and maple trees lined the broad avenues.

Again Janette's Diary tells us:

August 3.

"In the afternoon we had two interesting games of cro-quet, one lasting an hour and thirty five minutes ... Saturday morning we had a walk along the Willamette then took the train to Turner. Our object being to look for a house ... We learned there were three or four vacant houses in town so we began to choose and plan in our minds, but did not get much farther. After dinner Mr. S. and W. went to select one, W. telling me just as soon as we did that, we would measure for carpets, etc. But like the trick mule in the circus, which is always just going to do something but never getting it done, so one by one our hopes faded not to return for at least two weeks.

"Sunday had an audience of 93, very honest looking faces, more than at any point yet. Though other denom. have preach-ing service the Pres. draw the largest congregation. Received an invitation from Mr. Cornelius and Mrs. to spend our next visit there. In the afternoon we went to S.S. When we went in Mr. Robinson's little boy of about ten years was at the organ playing the chords for the different hymns. A hymn would be selected, the little fellow would wait until someone gave him the key of it then he started off. The Supt. gave out 'Yield not to Temptation.' Two ladies started, lagged and finally stopped altogether. We timidly went on, two ladies behind me with strong voices, took it up and carried it through, in spite of the black looks of ladies No. 1. At close of school Mr. Shaw asked me to play, I did so though I did not know the first hymn very well. One lady said she was glad we were coming, my voice would be such a help in singing. I learned that some half dozen different ladies could play but would not lest they should arouse jealousy. This knowledge made me feel as if 'They say' would accuse me of thrusting myself forward, but here Will comes in with his words of comfort and advice to pay no attention to Madam Grundy. This village I understand is preeminent in gossiping. How I dread living among people whose chief end is to know and tell what their neighbor is doing. Besides I must either learn to lead a conversation or listen to small talk.

"Monday morning we left word for Mr. McKinney to let us know when we could have possession of a house and returned to Mr. Voorhees' to wait! We were glad to get back to good-sized quarters again, our room at Shaws being of little larger dimensions than that of Condits. The only management we had was to get our heads high enough for comfort without a bolster, it occurred to Will that there was a roll of carpet under the bed so when we were nearly asleep he got up, lit a light, got it and fixed it under our pillows.

"On Sunday we saw two men hauling in straw, one taking a harvester along, another with two sewing machines, a man in working clothes come out of the saloon and start off in two-horse wagon."

August 9.

"Will has been out riding wih Mr. V. around Gervais and meeting some of the people. There are whole souled folks with simple manners. From listening he got these points. We must never talk of our neighbors at all or say ought of anyone except good because the people do little else but gossip. They want a great deal of visiting done and that too in most familiar way. We will have to learn to put up with their ways of doing things as though we had been used to them all our lives."

August 13.

"Will took a walk being very tired and I accompanied him to 'Lone Firs.' We got some beautiful moss which we mailed to Joel and Aunt Sarah."

August 14-17.

"No word in regard to house at Turner so Will went down next day but could not succeed any better himself so returned on afternoon train. But we resolved to come up and go to Mr. Cornelius: So Thurs. morn- we left bag and baggage. As we said good-bye to one and all that had been so kind to us it was with deep feeling that we seconded Mrs. V's remark that we must not forget this was our first Oregon home. Having been there from July 9th to August 16th it has become a place of rest and welcome to us.

"On getting off the train at Turner, Mr. Condit met us . . . Will went with Mr. Condit around to Mrs. Cromwell's to see if he could engage rooms. Mrs. C. just arrived on the same train we did from Tacoma and while with her five children she could not have everything just in order, she agreed to take us, so here we are and have been since yesterday afternoon. We take our meals across the street at Mr. Angus Shaw's . . .

"We saw the snow-covered mountains last evening for the first time since we have been in Oregon. As the sun illumined them at setting we enjoyed their beauty to the full."
August 20.

"Friday afternoon Mr. Henry Condit drove in for us and took us to Sylvanus Condits . . . Now we are here again with no prospect of house, this waiting is hard for us both, being idle tends to make us discontented. What changeable beings we are! We said we would be satisfied if we could only get rooms here. We had a much more enjoyable stay at Mr. C's. this time. Why? — Why we had chicken, *actual* not imaginary, toast, eggs, fruit and good rich milk. Sunday morning Will preached at Pleasant Grove to an audience of about fifty, several faces of those we met before were absent and yesterday a few new ones were present . . ."
August 21.

"We were glad to get the home letters for we had not heard for nine days owing to our leaving Woodburn and letters must be remailed. Will had a letter from Frisco stating that he had paid excess $13.10. If he would forward his address they would send it to him. He has a good word for R.R. now. We are taking our meals at Mr. Perry Cornelius' this eve we sat down to tea and Mr. C. picked up his napkin and fixed it on his lap. Mrs. was just asking Will to give thanks. Will did so. Mr. C. said, 'I beg your pardon Mr. Young, I forgot. We are accustomed to begin right away. I will try to conform to circumstances as best I can.' Nothing was said by anyone for several seconds when Will remarked, 'There is something very appropriate to me in acknowledging our gifts as we receive them.' Straws tell which way the wind blows."
August 22.

"About ten o'clock Cassius Cornelius came for us. The

three miles ride out there was rough and hilly much of it through thick fir forest, in a long rough lane to the house which is enclosed by hills. We had a pleasant afternoon nothing unusual occurred ...

"After dinner Will and Cassius went gunning, climbed around through the thick underbrush, carrying a heavy gun, that was so hard work that by the time Will would get the trigger pulled, he would have lost his aim. Finally Will fired one shot at a squirrel and Cassius another and would have knocked it in the head had not he slipped and fell. So much for his first gunning excursion in Oregon. Our bedroom was on the cage plan with bed, wee stand and box covered on which was bowl and pitcher, no soap, comb or brush, mirror or *needful*. Will went to the window to raise it, but it was nailed down so we left our door open into the parlor. The next morning each up and out W. to barn I to woodshed. We had hot bread and cakes and mutton that tasted of the animal until we were ready to cry quits. A sheep is laid on the chopping block and its head severed with an ax."
August 23.

"Thurs. afternoon it was proposed we visit Baker's, none of them being members except Mrs. (a baptist) and the reason being because there were so many young folks to be reached. We found them a very cordial entertaining family. They are pioneers came across the plain 32 years ago in an ox-cart. It was between the years the cholera took so many of the immigrants and Mrs. B. told of seeing dozens of bodies lying along the alkali plains. Our visit was pleasant we were treated to watermelon, pears, apples and plums, they like most of these westerners live bountifully."

The Bakers' farm was surrounded by a "snake fence" seven logs high. They still lived in a picturesque strong-built log cabin, with low solid walls of logs and an overhanging shingled roof. The big open fire-place and wide chimney looked homelike and inviting. By the side of the fire-place were two deer horns fastened to the wall, holding a rifle, and on the high mantel shelf stood the clock. Two corner cupboards held their supply of dishes. Next to the house was a storehouse for apples so that the smell of apples filled the whole house.

They invited Janette and Will to stay to dinner and served a

The Young family home, near Parkesburg, Pennsylvania, built in 1820. In the foreground, Ezekial Rambo Young and Sarah Parke Young. Behind them, Sister Fannie (third from left) and Sister Clara (extreme right).

PLEASANT GROVE

PRESBYTERIAN CHURCH
BEGAN WITH THE ARRIVAL
OF THE REVEREND PHILIP
CONDIT IN SEPTEMBER 1854.
THE CONGREGATION WAS OR-
GANIZED JANUARY 1, 1855.
THE BUILDING WAS COMPLET-
ED IN 1858. IT IS THE OLDEST
CHURCH BUILDING ERECTED
BY PRESBYTERIANS ON THE
PACIFIC COAST.

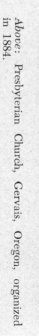

Above: Presbyterian Church, Gervais, Oregon, organized in 1884.

Above left: Historical plaque at Pleasant Grove Church.

Left: Presbyterian Church, Pleasant Grove, Oregon, built in 1858.

bountiful repast of roast pork, potatoes, vegetables and fresh apple pie. After dinner Mr. Baker put a big log in the fireplace, and told them of his experiences as a young man crossing the plains.

"What was Oregon like in those days?", Will asked.

"When we came here," said Mr. Baker, "this valley was like a big open prairie with red clover and native grasses stretching as far as eye could reach. There was fine hay for cattle before people began coming in to plough it up and spoil it. All this oak brush has grown up since. The trouble with Oregon is that there are too many homesteaders, too much cattle. Now all the wild life is disappearing."

Mrs. Baker told of the sickness they had to contend with, when nearly every family lost some loved one. After all those years, her eyes filled with tears as she told of the death of her baby girl, and how hard it was to leave her dear one buried in that lonely grave in the desert sands. They had started with fine furniture, — chairs, table and dresser. But one piece after another had to be discarded along the way. She proudly showed them a little rocking chair, the only piece of furniture that she had been able to save. When they left to go home, the Bakers gave them apples, pears, and a smoked ham.

Janette wrote:

August 23.

"We returned safely to Mr. Cornelius after the nervousness of riding behind a two year old colt not accustomed to single harness and a wagon with a broken shaft."

Will wrote in Janette's Diary:

"Last night in writing Mother Lewis I enclosed a few receipts gleaned by eyesight mainly on this visit. To comb yr. hair: — wet it well and let it alone, or leave it unwet and alone as most handy. To mend yr. shirt: — Put another one on top. To keep chickens out of the yard: — have a gate with at least two panels out of it. To have a fence look neat: — whitewash where it shows thus preserve looks and save whitewash. To obtain a teakettle easily: — Get an old iron boiler and call it a kettle."

Janette wrote:

August 24.

"Lizzie and Ariadne brought us in to Turner where we found people already knew we are intending to buy Mr. Blakeney's house and Mr. C. told us we were quite likely to get it. It will take us a long time to get used to everybody knowing all that concerns us."

August 25.

"This morning the answer was that the house was taken by a gentleman who had first chance. Will offered him $350 cash for the one he was living in or was willing to rent it. Mr. B. held it at $400 but let W. have it at his offer. We went over and measured it and wrote home about it."

So at last they found the little white frame house that Mr. Condit had told them about, and it suited them well. It had a parlor, dining room, kitchen and three bedrooms, and also a study that could house Will's fine collection of over 500 volumes. The house stood three feet above the ground because of Oregon's long spells of dampness. They would have to build a woodshed.

Janette especially loved the view of the distant hills covered with fir trees, and just back of their lot were the woods where they could gather wild flowers and berries.

"Now" said Janette proudly, "this is really and truly our own home."

At once they went over and measured the floors for carpets and the windows for curtains.

August 30.

"Mon. morn we took the early train to Woodburn. Newtie met us, took us home where we had a cordial welcome. Knowing Mr. Voorhees had had experience Will asked him how to secure a clear title to the place he had bought. Mr. V. told him to get a Warrantee Deed signed by both Mr. Blakeney and wife and then have it immediately recorded. All of which he did yesterday in Salem in the presence of Mr. Crawford, so we are residents of Turner, Oregon, USA., N.A. Monday we went to Portland to buy furniture. Will and I went out to an auction store, found a second hand bed-lounge could be had for twenty-five dollars. A new one costs forty. We went to a carpet establishment. No brussels carpet under a dollar, heavy cardinal curtains on which we had set our hearts were twelve dollars a pair.

"We then went to another store, found we could get white muslin and cardinal flannel for but twenty cents per yard. On the way home Will was speechless, in spite of the public eye.

I took a hearty laugh over the thoughts of how the money would hold out at that rate!

"We priced things at several stores, determined to get a good article for the least money. Finally we came to Mr. Powers to whom Mr. Rutherford had given Will a letter of introduction. We found we could and did do better there than at any other places. Will got ten and in some things, twenty per cent off. It was a busy day. After a good night's rest we returned to Salem, bargained for the house and bought our hardware from Mr. Crawford. He was so kind, had me tell how all the tin ware etc. I wanted so I will be well provided for in the culinary department... Then I went back to the Crawfords and lay down for a rest. Soon Will ran in for me saying he wanted me to go with him to look at a wagon which he had been told was a bargain. We went and agreed it was, so Will made an offer on it."

After they had bought their wagon, he bought a horse whom they named Prince. They bought lumber for the woodshed and book shelves, had it loaded on the wagon and then drove back to Turner.

Will wrote, after a trip to Stayton:

September 3.

"It was quite late, more than 7:30 when I got in... when I came to the room Janette had the *Valley Union* pinned up in a conspicuous place with my account of our trip from Chicago to Ogden in it."

Janette continued:

"Mrs. Cornelius made me the offer of using her stove to preserve fruit, accordingly, this forenoon, I, by her kindness and also Mrs. Cromwell's in giving me cans, cooked the dollars worth (3 gallons) blackberries bought on Saturday and had nearly a gallon canned, two quarts of jam and two cups of jelly. But the customary term for jelly here is 'jell,' both noun and verb.

"Will subscribed for the Oregonian.

"Yesterday he preached twice here at Turner. In the morning he had a fair attendance, 65 but like all meetings, is smaller this time of the year owing to the visiting on Sunday and the threshing done that day. In the morning we saw a man hauling a load of tanning bark."

Janette and Will worked hard to get their little home in readiness, but it was a labor of love. They were happy to know that this was to be their home. Janette made curtains of the white muslin and the cardinal canton flannel. When they had put them up, their little home looked very cozy. They unpacked their boxes and put the books on the shelves that Will had made in their study.

Janette's Dairy had only one entry:

September 18.

"Too tired to write."

She continued:

September 19.

"Will at his study I beside him happy in our own little home. Over and over again have told each other how happy we are, what a satisfaction to feel we are not renting and likely to be obliged to move. Last friday Mr. McNeill, Mr. Thompson and four others helped move the piano [a square grand] in. Mr. Thompson a very strong man would make speeches such as, 'Oh, look at my dirty face in the creetur' and while the others could not lift for laughing he was still himself strong. Sat. morning as we were working away the door-bell rang and Mr. Robinson came in saying he forgot it in the morning but they wanted Will to make an address at the funeral of Mr. Bowers services at the grave leave the house at two o'clock. It was then half-past eleven so we hurried around, Will worrying all the time that they had neglected to tell him in reasonable time. By two we were at the house — the corpse was brought outside for the friends to take leave the house being small and then put not in a hearse but a livery team wagon a long carriage with red running gears. Mr. Bowers died the day previous at noon. We were an hour and a half in going and the sun beat us all the way and in the graveyard a gentleman had to hold an umbrella over Will. The children were sore grieved over the separation one son crying 'gone, gone' and he the son so prayed over by his mother during her life but who is still on the downward road."

When they were all settled, their little home was comfortable and attractive. In the evenings Janette often sat down at the piano and played and sang the songs and hymns that they loved. Will joined her in singing, her contralto blending with his tenor, and they had great happiness.

They spent much time in the little study where a wood stove threw out a steady heat. While Will worked on his sermons or read, Janette sewed or wrote in her diary of the events of her daily life. There was a sofa in the study, and if she were tired she loved to lie down and have Will read to her. On a little stand stood one of their prized possessions, a large illustrated Bible, with dictionary and concordance, bound in brown leather with decorations and lettering in gold. It was a wedding present and on the fly leaf was written in her father's fine handwriting, "To Jennie and Will from Father and Mother, May 11, 1883." It was from this Bible that they often read.

From their childhood, when they had few children's books, "Pilgrims Progress" had become their favorite book. They often referred to Christian and Christiana and their progress to the Celestial City. The slough of despond was very real, and so were the Giant Despair and the Doubting Castle. They were glad of Hopeful, Faithful and Mr. Valiant for Truth.

When Janette planted the chrysanthemum slips that Sister Fannie had sent her, she told Will that she had planted some of the "Herb called Heartease" along with them.

They went out into the woods and dug up ferns and transplanted them to her garden. Under her care, the scraggly roses flourished. Will was pleased to see the roses blooming in her cheeks as well. Janette was very gay and happy and sang about her work indoors and out. The warm sunshine seemed to do her good and the cough that had bothered her back in Pennsylvania seemed a thing of the past.

One day Mr. Cornelius called. "I want to warn you," he said to Will, "the Baptist minister has gotten himself talked about by putting his arm around the girls."

"No danger," said Will laughing, "Janette would never stand for that."

In the first of Will's articles on "Impressions of Oregon," written for the folks at home and published in the Valley *Union* of West Chester, Pennsylvania, January 5, 1885, he said:

"A resident of the Willamette Valley for many months, it occurs to me some facts regarding this section of the Northwest may not be wholly uninteresting.

"The valley extends up south from the Columbia river to the Callapola mountains, 150 miles, and is from 30 to 60 miles in width; is bounded on the east by the Cascade range and on the west by the Coast range. It contains about 5,000,000 acres of land. The Willamette river flows through the centre, giving the name. There are two railroads in the valley, one completed through the valley and the other being pushed toward completion. A third railroad, a narrow gauge, has proved, up to the present, a not very good investment, as it has not been established in the section intended to be tapped by it.

"Great sections of the valley are deeply wooded. In some places there is 'scrub' growth, which has grown up within the memory of many of the Pioneers. It was the habit of the Indians to burn off large portions of the country yearly. When the burnings ceased soon luxuriant growths of plants and trees sprung up. The valley as a whole is made up of smaller valleys, or as they call them 'prairies.' The land is rolling and in many places, no stones at all are to be found, in other large sections they are very plentiful. The soil is almost without exception rich. No fertilizers are used. After threshing the straw is regularly burnt. The country is pretty largely taken up. Many of the residents have been here since 1842, and most of this class have large tracts of land.

"The farms are large, a quarter section (160 acres) or even a half section (320 acres), is held to be a small farm, 640 acres is very commonly the size, and I know of several farmers who have from 1000, 1500 and 2000 acres. Large portions of their farms are often covered with valuable timber, as fir, pine, oak and ash, but timber being abundant frequently the timber is 'slashed' and as soon as dry enough is burnt as it lies. The more usual clearing process is by grubbing. When cleared the plow is put into the soil and the farming begins. A field has often more than 200 acres of one kind of grain, generally wheat. The equipment of a farm in buildings is very light. The mild winters make the eastern barn unnecessary, stock are unsheltered all year. A shed to put away a little hay and to keep some horses and cows for convenience, with a corner in which you can drive a 'hack' is all that is usual.

"But there is a change going on in this direction and more care is being taken of animals and of machinery. Houses rarely have a cellar, the rainy season would but make a basin of it. In consequence of this houses are built on props from two to five feet above the ground. The farmer's house rarely has a brick or stone foundation. The farmer himself is a genial, often careless man, generally an excellent liver. If a pioneer, he loves to talk of his experience crossing the plains in his ox team, his narrow escapes from Indians, the difficulty of fording water, the sickness they had to contend with, and now and then the burial of a dear one in the desert sands, the giving out of horses and mules, the unloading, taking apart and carrying over certain steep places of the wagons and contents, the walking for great distances on foot, and when you are seated with him by his fire-place—your face burning and your back chilly —he will put on a big back log and some pitch fir in front, and then begin to talk in an Oregonian dialect, made up of ancient distorted eastern localisms, Indian and Chinese jargon, Americanized French and Spanish, and some English elements, of the trials and tribulations of pioneer life. Days when exchange of commodities was the order of the day and money was rare, when there were no roads or fences and neighbors very scarce. His family is usually large—one fellow-townsman has seventeen children.

"The towns in this valley are small but do a great deal of business. There are some peculiarities of trading that at first perplex a new comer. No pennies are used, nothing smaller than a nickle, and this is local, in many places dimes are the smallest change ... A quarter dollar alone would suffice, anything smaller is called 'chicken feed.' (It is impossible to have a collection of pennies out here). I have shown many an Oregonian his first penny. A dime is a short bit, and 15 cents a long bit. Sugar, calico, & c., are sold by the dollar's worth and every sort of produce by the pound.

"The regular life of the Oregonian is spasmodic. He has to make his hay when the sun shines, and then he works hard, but when the rain falls he takes things very easy."

V. Laborers for the Lord

Janette worked hard, getting their house in order, making calls with Will, writing letters home, and preparing for guests. She admitted that she had not kept up her Diary:

October 12.

"Nearly a month has elapsed and the pen has not responded to the call of the empty pages but today it should be recorded. Will worked hard this morning piling wood in the shed which is as yet without a roof and door. After we had dinner Will left for Gervais to visit around and preach. I could not accompany him as Mr. and Mrs. Murgatroyd are with us came last Thurs. eve. we find them pleasant, companionable friends. Mrs. has not been well and today had a chill, change of climate goes hard with her. On better acquaintance I retain the good impression I had of him at our wedding, is like Will good and kind to his wife.

"Dinner over, dressed, some mending done when bell rang. The Misses Cole came to call was more favorably impressed with them than I had hoped to be, . . . found them very lady-like and agreeable, had my mind relieved by Cassie saying she would play the organ for Pres. service.

"An uncle of theirs has just arrived in Portland came in 5 days over N.P. from Chicago to Portland . . . Mr. M. and Will went to Independence found a church organization 19 members — neat little ch. large town, 4 S.S. many stores. Independence is just opposite us across the river (air line about 8 mi. but actual distance by way of Salem 16 mi.) They had an experience crossing the ferry, the ferryman took quarter going over and in return they handed him two dimes and a nickel. 'Is that all the money you got? If it is keep it. I've no use for anything less than a quarter.' So they meekly handed him a half dollar and he gave change . . .

"Mrs. C. gave us some grapes, tomatoes, squash and watermelon. I made some good grape butter.

"Our little home is comfortable enough for us now, though we have worked hard—the first day I washed and we had dinner off Ches. Co. [Chester County] dried beef and milk biscuit though the oven would not bake well. I have succeeded with cooking beyond my expectations, had the pleasure of Will's telling me he did not know he was getting so good a cook—he is patient though when I spoil flour. Have had to feed three cakes to the pigs and we feared their teeth needed sharpening afterwards. Mrs. Potts irons do good work. Cinnamon and pepper being bought in little tin boxes I used one for the other."

Will had just come in and found her flushed from cooking over the hot stove. In her excitement, just as she had taken an apple pie from the oven, the crust golden brown and the apples smelling delectable, having sprinkled it with sugar, she took what she thought was the cinnamon can and sprinkled it generously, only then realizing that she had taken the pepper can by mistake.

"Oh, Will," she cried, "just see what I have done! My beautiful pie is ruined!"

"Oh never mind, dear, we will just scrape off the pepper and it will be as good as ever," and together they laughed over her error. The Diary continues:

"We undertook to paper the study, cut paper, got paste on it, tried to fasten it to ceiling but the perverse stuff fell off at one end as fast as we stuck it at the other. Mr. Cornelius called to see us was our first guest at meals. As he sat in the big sofa rocker he said, 'Ah, Mr. Young you're a man after my own heart.'

"Mrs. Cyrenus Condit stopped here on her way home from Presby. I showed her the bread so nice and light, she sighed, 'so many of 'em don't know how' (meaning ministers' wives.)

"Eleven o'clock, so good night, good friend!"
October 13.

"Today while in midst of my sweeping an old man walked in. I gave him a seat and soon learned he was hunting his son-in-law Charles Cannon. Thought this was Blakeney's, but knowing he was very tired I kept him and talked to him, learned he was from Wayne Co., Penn. left there in '38 went to Iowa, came overland to Oregon in '48. lives 12 mi. from here with his daughter . . .

"Being deaf I had to talk loud to make him hear. Mr. and

Mrs. Murgatroyd in their room had the benefit of· the conversation. But it was an event to me to meet a man who had frequently been in Phila. when it was an infant town.

"This afternoon I called on Mrs. Porter saw her young baby, which has a head of hair black as mine . . .

"Letter from Joel today full of christian fellowship and comfort.

"Saturday night, ending of a more than busy week! Blessed be the sabbath of rest weekly reminder that one day of rest is needful."
October 29.

"We drove to Salem today in less than two hours, though thus late in October we were not cold because it was dull and rainy. We saw a number of Chinese and Indians, nothing unusual here though . . .

"Last Wed. week 17th we drove to Marion leaving Mr. and Mrs. M. in charge of affairs, we visited a number of families Mrs. Rutherford accompanied us and introduced us. Will must have made a favorable impression on Grandmother Hendricks for yesterday Mr. Rutherford gave him a pair of mittens that Grandma had knit for him (Will) rather they are gloves, doubly thick, and represent the rainbow, if the rainbow could be cut into pieces and arranged like a kaliedoscope, but Will is satisfied, they will just suit to drive in and will last for years.

"We called on a family living in the house where Mr. Rutherford brought his bride. 'Hotel Bismark' they dub it. Newspapers on the walls for paper, holes in the door covered with paper, stairway almost perpendicular."
November 6.

"On our return from Marion while Will put the horse way, I went into S.S. just got there in time to teach Miss Dennier's class and play the organ. Being such a stormy day Mr. Shaw did not intend to announce Praise Service for the evening, but I told him Will was on hand and I knew wanted to have it. 'All right,' he said and so announced it. So in the eve. we were gratified to see not the staid church going people as usual but quite a number of men who are not churchgoers. Everyone seemed to enjoy the singing too.

"The week following was very busy, I went to Mrs. Cromwell's and hemmed napkins while she read Chatuaqua Magazine aloud I am a member of the C. Li. S.C. [Chatauqua Literary Scientific Circle]." That circle, organized in 1878 for home study, had grown so that in the first year 7,000 persons were enrolled."

The Diary continues:

November 14.

"Will was hurried as he wrote a missionary sermon to deliver Sunday morning and a talk for Sat. afternoon preparatory service and another sermon for Sunday eve. His first Communion Service! How anxious he was to have everything done carefully and indeed he did show that it was not in his own but his Master's strength, and we all received good from the day's privileges and precious communion. But what with housework and extra sewing and calls made and callers entertained I was so worried, I was just discouraged but by perseverances and taking fresh courage I came safely along through all. Yesterday we went ... to Coles to dinner—they remind us of Eastern folks. Mrs. Cole is like Mother Latta ...

"After dinner drove to Whitsels. Mrs. W. is a member of Presbyterian Church. We had a pleasant time, saw Mrs. W. spinning or rather carding wool, a novel sight to us! Came home, had tea, and Will wrote a number of letters while I ironed."

Janette admired the work Mrs. Whitsel was doing, and asked her when she had learned to card and spin.

"I came here across the plains when I was a child, and was married when I was fifteen," she said. "And by then I knew how to card the wool, spin it into thread, weave the cloth, and make it up into clothes. I remember how proud I was of the first suit I made for my husband.

"We lived in a little log cabin. I cooked over a mud fireplace, but so did everybody else. So I didn't know I was having a hard time. I baked all my bread and biscuit in an iron skillet with a lid, set on stones in the fireplace. To make them brown, I put coals on top. I kept busy making soap, knitting socks, and looking after the babies.

"My husband took a half section of land. We've done well, and a few years ago built this house. But I still card and spin and weave because I like to. It seems like the young girls now-a-days don't want to learn."

Janette kept busy all day long with housework, sewing and entertaining callers and making calls.

"Sometimes, Will, I feel I am too busy to do the Lord's work. Just the daily tasks are all I can do."

"But dear, that is all God asks of any of us, just to do our best even if the tasks are humble."

"But Will, you have your work and each week more people are coming to the church, but sometimes I feel so useless, I wish that I had something to do that would make me feel that I belonged here."

One day as Janette had just finished "picking up the house," in came Mrs. Rutherford, Mrs. Neal, Mrs. Condit, Mrs. Riches, Mrs. Shaw, Mrs. Cromwell and Mrs. Cornelius. Mrs. Rutherford was the spokesman.

"Mrs. Young," she said, "we want to form a missionary society and we want you to be our president."

Janette was secretly pleased. "Why, I do appreciate your asking me. Do you think I could do it?"

Just then Will came in. "What is going on here?" he asked. They explained their errand and said, "We want to call it 'The Women's Missionary Society of the Presbyterian Church of Turner' and we want your wife to be president because everyone likes her."

Will led in prayer, read a passage from the scripture and helped them form their constitution.

Luckily Janette had baked a cake that morning, and the tea kettle was boiling, so in no time she served tea. In that social hour they all got better acquainted.

After they had gone, Will put his arm around her affectionately, "Now Madame President, I guess you will really feel that you belong in Turner."

Janette wrote in her Diary:
November 17.

"Last Wed. we drove to Independence. Mr. Murgatroyd was ordained in eve. Dr. Lindsley preached sermon — Mr. Condit preached Thurs. eve. Mr. Lee Fri. eve. They, Mr. and Mrs., like their new place very well . . .

"Independence is a western boom town, has grown within 7 yrs. Buildings are substantial and pretty—3 storied school building, two churches, large hotel, opera house, all kinds of stores etc. We were pleased with our trip...

"We left Frid. morn, drove to Salem, 11½ mi., got lunch, on to Gervais, 17 mi. Made call on Mrs. Clark (a girl wife) on to our 1st Or. home. Harry and May danced when they saw us and indeed we had a delightful visit, sang, played with the children, talked, read and on Sat. we called at Halls where we saw Grandmother H. knitting fine thread lace and tidies. Called at Hunsukers just as we stopped their horses ran away with the plough. Mr. H. broke out with an oath and afterward apologized saying 'he didn't know there was a lady in the wagon.' We saw an Illinois apple which made us think of home. Called at Riddles though Mrs. takes in washing hers was one of the neatest houses we were in. Then we returned to Voorhees tired and glad to be in out of the rain."
November 19.

"Sun. morn Will preached from Text 'How shall we escape if we neglect so great salvation?' As soon as ch. was over an old lady in front of me jumped up with 'There I wish the lower school could hear that.' I was in a quandry. Mrs. V. introduced us. I asked 'did you like the sermon?' 'Yes,' she said, 'That's right, tell him to preach Jesus.' She is the lady who is related to nearly everyone around. Whitsel's school house (Mrs. Whitsel) and through whom the S.S. was organized there this summer. Mr. Voorhees Supt.

"In the afternoon we left for Gervais with bag of buckwheat, 7 jars fruit, dried apples, Mrs. Rice is so kind.

"As I sat in ch. at Ger. I could look out at snow capped Mt. Hood glistening in the sun light... We drove home as far as Salem went to ch. heard an excellent sermon by Mr. Berry and went home with Van Eatons... We had a homelike visit, they have two sweet children. Will looked happy when he got one on either knee. Maggie asked her mama if Mr. Y. preached. Mrs. V. said no he heard Mr. Berry preach. 'Why mama does he think Mr. Berry a *bright star?*' We came home Mon. at noon—passed an old man on the way horseback—he rode up to the house, said he thought he recognized us at ch. last eve. Will said we were. He introduced himself as Mr. McFadden had a pleasant chat and rode on...

"Have just seen a fearful sight, Will calls 'runaway team.'

We rush to the door in time to see them dash down the road and as they neared the bridge Will hallos 'they are fast together and down they will go.' No sooner said than they struck the bridge, slipped and both tumbled over into the stream. The owner after on a dead run too late though to save them. A crowd of men hasten to the scene.

"Fortunately recess was over, children just been called in.

"11:30 Will back, says horse No. 1 fell as he struck the bridge, jumped up, that made No. 2 slip and he fell in pulling No. 1 after him. The stream Mill Creek is high at this season and a very swift stream. Down they floated until tangled in some bushes. The men gathered round, got near enough to cut the rope that held them together, got one out, the other they said was drowned, the man went in the water to it, got its head above water, it began to breathe, to pant and to snort and in its scrambling kicked the man out into the stream, he floated though swimming all the time, the others tried to throw him a rope and finally succeeded in getting it to him and saving him. Others still pulled and worked till they got the other horse out though poor thing was nearly scared to death, stood snorting and trembling and as they brought the dripping horses back to town, their eyes looked wild. They have blanketed them and are exercising them. I trust the man is being properly taken care of . . ."

November 23.

"Neglected work means double duty now. On Nov. 20th, Tuesday, we attended Miss Denyer's wedding. The bride and groom were teachers at the same time in Turner. There were present all of Mr. Denyer's family and Mr. Smith's mother and sister and her husband and two or three others. Just as Will was about to pronounce the words that would put them in misery, or rather ask the question if anyone had any objection to their union, Mrs. D's baby cried, so the ceremony was deferred for a few minutes till the Mother gave her little one that which quiets all babies. Then the ceremony proceeded after which we had dinner. Soon the bride left for her new home, the wagon containing Mr. Smith's brother-in-law and wife in front seat, Mrs. Smith senior and junior on back seat, and the happy groom sitting on the floor behind. Thus they rode up through Turner."

On Thanksgiving Day Janette decorated the church with big sprays of oats and ferns for the service. She wanted to surprise Will and had a hard time doing it. But it did her good to see Will look so pleased as he walked up the church aisle. He chose the first verse of the 107th Psalm as the text for his sermon: "Oh give thanks unto the Lord for He is good and His mercy endureth forever."

They were invited to the Shaws to dinner. As this was their first Thanksgiving away from their dear ones it is no wonder that they were a bit homesick with longing. As they drove out into the country after church they recalled all that Thanksgiving had meant to them at home. Their last Thanksgiving in Pennsylvania had been an especially happy occasion. Janette had come home from Springdale, where she was teaching school, and Will from Union Theological Seminary. The whole Lewis family had been invited to dinner by the Young family at Fairview Farm. They met at Upper Octorara Church, and Will managed it so that he and Janette would have a little time to themselves before the service began. When they arrived home after church, half famished, they had been greeted by the delicious fragrance of pumpkin and mince pies and roasting turkey. Fannie was ten years older than Will and Clara was six years older. Will always spoke of them as "the girls." They were both acknowledged as excellent cooks. The table was stretched out at full length. Fannie, the artistic one, had decorated it with autumn leaves and chrysanthemums. What a merry time they had! Janette's brother, Clifford, was a great one for jokes and kept them all laughing.

How different it all was this year! But they told themselves over and over how much they had to be thankful for. The fact that they could be together and that she could share in Will's work was Janette's special cause for thankfulness, and Will said that having such a dear and loving wife was his. It was a dull day. The bare and leafless trees stood out against the fir and pine trees. Only the scrub oak clung to its thick brown leaves. The flowers of the goldenrod and aster showed some color in the fence corners and the brick red spikes of the sumachs still glowed. Many of the birds had gone south for the winter, but not all. Saucy blue jays called to them from the bare trees, and tree sparrows, chicadees and finches foraged for weed seeds along the side of the road.

"I must remember to put out some grain for my birds," said Janette. "I want them to have a happy Thanksgiving too."

Janette's Diary tells of a Donation Party:

November 30.

"We came home Thanksgiving Day about four o'clock, fixed up the house, while Will fed Prince. Then we sat in the study and Will read aloud. He seemed low spirited and I had not energy enough to entertain him but knew all would be gay in an hour. He kept asking if I were not going to choir practice. I said, 'No hurry, Mrs. McKinney never goes till the train comes.' Will had one more page to read then intended to fix the fire and take me over when the door-bell rang and Mr. Lindsey and Mr. Miller came in. Presently we heard voices outside. Will looked at me and winked as much as to say, 'There's something up.' I answered with a wink as if it was all new to me. The doorbell rang again and there before Will stood a whole crowd with baskets, boxes, bundles and bags of oats. In the midst was Johnny Cole with a live pig in a box. Recovering from his surprises, Will set to work to entertain the kind-hearted crowd. And a good time they had as each one testified afterwards. The whole house was thrown open and different games were carried on with plenty of fun and laughter. Mr. Thomas came in his shirt sleeves, carrying a bag of oats, told me I could use it for cakes. Old Mr. Johnson, Mr. Cannon's father was hauled around in a wheelbarrow. He is 83 years old. His legs are partially paralyzed. Poor old man he was so glad to be noticed that he cried. He knew places Will mentioned in Chester County."

Janette sat down at the big square piano and a crowd of young people gathered round to sing the popular songs. She and Will caused much laughter when they sang, "Reuben, Reuben, I've been thinking," and then "I'm Romeo, I'm Juliet." Some hadn't realized that their young minister had so much fun in him.

Some of the boys sang to the tune of "Oh, Susanna!"

"I came from Salem City
With my wash bowl on my knee
I am going to California
The gold dust for to see.
It rained all night the day I left
The weather it was dry

The sun so hot I froze to death
Oh! brother don't you cry.
Oh! California .
That's the land for me.
I'm going to Sacramento
With my wash bowl on my knee."

The newspaper of December gave a report of the donation party:

"Last Thursday evening Rev. W. S. Young and wife were agree-
ably surprised by many of their friends of this place, going there
en masse for a donation visit . . . Mr. Young came from Pennsylvania
last July. He is a gentleman highly educated and has a choice
library of five hundred fifty well selected volumes. Mrs. Young is
very much of a lady and she and Mr. Young have gained many
friends."

Janette's Diary tells us:

"Refreshments were passed around soon after which the
folks left, not to go off to a dance however. Just the things
were brought which were useful. In all some 2 cans of fruit,
cabbage, beets, turnips, roast chicken, two live ones, butter,
sugar, and apples."

This donation party made quite a vivid impression on William
Stewart Young, since in undated notes he wrote about it many years
later:

"The pig became a source of contention as it made it
necessary for us to go home always at night to feed it, so we
could not stay when night caught us calling. But eventual-
ly . . . we sold it to the Chinaman who worked on the railroad.
And this reminds me that all the farmers when they killed their
fall pigs would bring us spare ribs, sausage, scrapple, and what
not galore . . . It spoiled on our hands so that one day we loaded
it all into the buggy and going out to a lone place near the
roadway through the woods, threw it out with a feeling of
relief."

When Will and Janette had arrived at Turner in mid-1883,
the little old building of the Presbyterian Church was in a sad state
of repair. It was dirty and in need of paint. The spire had blown
down in a windstorm, and there was no money to replace it.

"Do you know, Will," she said, "Mrs. Rutherford told me that
the Methodists pass the collection basket every Sunday. But of
course the Presbyterians would never come to that."

"The church certainly needs fixing up," said Will, "but I don't know where the money is coming from."

Janette decided to call a meeting of the Women's Missionary Society, for, as she said, "Missions should certainly begin at home."

They decided to have a work week. The women washed the windows, cleaned and scrubbed, and the men came in and gave the woodwork a coat of clean white paint. After that the women had a "Missionary Tea," to earn money to repair the spire. They worked with a will and, by Christmas, the little church stood clean and white, with its new spire.

The young people helped decorate the church. The boys went out into the woods and brought back a Christmas tree, and branches of pine, fir, spruce and holly berries. The girls of Janette's Sunday School class wove these into garlands and wreaths. The Christmas service was held on Sunday, December 23. Janette had trained her class to sing the Christmas carols: "Oh, Little Town of Bethlehem" and "Hark the Herald Angels Sing." So the Christmas time that she had dreaded was a happy one. As she looked around at the church with its evergreen decorations and the Christmas tree sparkling with many candles, she put aside a wave of homesickness. She concentrated on her young husband, as he read the Christmas story and preached the sermon on the text found in Matthew 11, 2, "We have seen His star in the east and are come to worship Him."

Letters from home told of Christmas preparations. Mother Young wrote that the girls were busy cracking walnuts and seeding raisins, getting ready to make their famous fruit cake. It seemed to Will and Janette that they could almost smell the spicy odors as the fruit cake baked. The letters told of a Christmas box that was to be sent with gifts from the two families. Janette's mother wrote that her brother Clifford would go up into the hills above their farm to cut a Christmas tree. On other years Janette had always been with him to help select the most symmetrical one. Then together they trimmed it with much fun and laughter as they put on strings of popcorn and cranberries. But they had little time to spend in self-pity. They looked forward with eagerness to the arrival of the Christmas box. Every time Will went to the post-office he would enquire whether it had come, only to be told, "Not yet."

Janette wrote in her Diary:

December 27.

"These are busy days for Will, first a week's meeting here,

then over to Spring Valley to assist Mr. Murgatroyd, back again two evenings here, then the rest of the week at Pleasant Grove. Then up to Marion three nights there. The work at Marion is hard because so few people to work upon . . . Mr. McCullough of Marion intends to give 'two bits a time,' as he says 'for every time Will preaches there.'

"Monday 24th December, I went to Marion on the eleven o'clock train, it poured rain all day and I did not get out anywhere. In the evening there was a public tree in the school house at which folks had a good time. Old Santa brought me a box of perfumery. Mrs. Rutherford gave me a combination suit, bottle of perfumery, tie and ruche and apron made of linen, 60 years old. I took train home next morn. Came to Thomas' stayed for breakfast, was asked to return thanks. Came over home and wrote home. Will came on 11 o'clock [train], had been to Gervais to make an address at Christmas S.S. entertainment Christmas eve. Had a crowded house, two trees good singing, nice presents. He was presented with a purse containing $11.50 — I received a box from ladies of Gervais containing 21 jars fruit and jelly. Will was asked to speak at Woodburn but could not as it was at the same hour.

"Well, Christmas at noon we drove out to Mr. Hilleary's through more water than I am used to. The heavy rain and snow melting had swollen the streams till they overflowed their banks and the mill race road was one sheet of water and part of the road bed washed away. I was very much alarmed. We reached there had a nice dinner. Days and Millers were there. Mrs. Day and Will had quite a time playing jokes on each other which furnished sport for the rest of the crowd. We came home, I with a sick headache had to go to bed and leave Will on Christmas night. There was a party at Coles for which big preparations had been made but Will, dear good fellow would not go without me, so denied himself and spent the evening in loneliness writing letters to old chums, thereby giving vent to his lonely feelings. But at train time, ever thoughtful went out and bought me some oranges which did taste good."

Christmas came and went and still no box. Each day they had looked for it to come.

"Why do you suppose it is so late?" asked Janette.

"You must remember it has a long way to come, and the mail is always slow at Christmas time."

Will had to go back to Marion so Janette went to Cromwells to stay all night. Her Diary of January 2, 1884, telling of events of December 27, says:

"I found that there was to be a surprise party there and did not want to stay as had no invitation. Mrs. C. insisted and when the others came found Mrs. Cornelius had sent Georgie over to invite me but I was away. Had a pleasant eve. Charades especially good—but dancing and eucher playing spoiled it for me. Mrs. Cromwell asked me to join the singing to drown the dancing, the idea! Singing gospel hymns to drown that!

"Next morn I came home to find smoke coming out of the chimney. Found Will had returned on 6 A.M. train. The long looked for box from Parkesburg had at last arrived. He had hauled the box home had it partly unpacked then waited on me . . .

"Oh! what rejoicing there was as one after another things were brought out showing the handiwork of the dear ones. We knelt and thanked God for His great love toward us in giving us such homes and such relatives. We do pray for more consecration for greater willingness and ability to work for God. We pray for blessings for those dear ones. I can best tell what the box contained by quoting the paper found in it."

"*Contents of Missionary box*: packed on November 24th at Fairview Farm near Parkesburg, for Turner, Oregon:

"Shoes for Will and Janette from Father Young. He hopes they will fit. A pair of blankets from Mother Young. She hopes you will be warm under them. A rug from Brother Thomas. He hopes you will not get too much Oregon mud on it before he sees it again. Apron for Janette from Sister Clara and a pair of gloves for Will. Pocket handkerchiefs for Jennie and Will from Sister Fannie. 'Try and keep your noses clean.'

"A box of Rio coffee (it looks awful good) and a box of candy from Mother and Father Lewis. They say Will likes candy, Jennie, don't let him have all of it.

"Pillow cases from sister Annie. 'Pleasant dreams.'

"Package from Father, Mother and family.

"A book of poetry from Clifford.

"An apron from Aunt Margaret. She says to wash dishes in it. A pair of mittens from Aunt Frank. Tidy from Aunt Mary. Pillow shams from Fannie and Clara.

"A box of home made candles. A can of honey to eat on your buckwheat cakes. A bolster to make into pillows. A sofa pillow. A pillow for sofa pillow, feathers bought of Mrs. Weaver. She said she was glad she had feathers to put in it for us. Mother did not sew it up, thought you would want some for other cushion. A fruit cake — Chestnuts from Aunt Margaret. We put in a few dried cherries, pears, and lima beans so that you could have a Chester County dinner.

"Here is a bag of gladiolas and tuberose bulbs for you, Janette.

"With much love from Young and Company."

Janette expressed her pleasure by writing in her Diary:

"We immediately wrote to them endeavoring to show our appreciation. Telling Mother that the blankets will laugh at the dampness of Oregon, telling how beautiful Thomas' rug is, and how we wish that he would soon come and see it and that not much mud would get on it. That the feather edge on apron reminds me of the hours I used to sit working on it. The gloves are more respectable looking than the kaleidoscope ones given him by Grandmother Hendricks. We will carefully keep the handkerchief seventeen years old of Em. Patton's brother who was studying for the ministry. The box of coffee was candy and Will carried it round under his arm munching every now and then and in the meantime crying for nuts. Nice bolster case from home and towels of Mrs. Newlin and bag of shelled, shell barks and bag of chestnuts.

"The pillow shams are beautiful. The feathers from Weaver's make me long to see the dear old farm. The fruit cake is a familiar sight to Will. The shoes also, he has gotten a new pair every Christmas for years. A cushion, all except top came in box. The top we received Friday January 11th. Fannie had sent it around to Parkes, Rings, Micheners, Thorndale, West Chester, each one worked some design, then Fannie filled it out and sent it along. It kept us 1 hour late for dinner. Mrs. Hilleary was here we had to examine and talk over the work. It has been much admired by folks here."

Will wrote in Janette's Diary:

"New Years Eve. The close of a very eventful year, a year to which we had looked forward for a long while and one we will always look back to with kindest feelings to those with whom we have worked. A year that has seen the culmination of more fond hopes than any one year's experience. A year possibly containing the key to life's possibilities for us."

Janette wrote on January 2, 1884:

"We went to the Cornelius' home to dinner on New Year's Day. There were a number of other guests present. After dinner Will went home to attend to the fires. He soon returned and handed me a paper on which was written: 'A glad New Year and compliments of ... [then followed the signatures of twenty of the church people]. It was all an enigma to me. The ladies made me wait until they got ready to accompany me home, in the meantime pretending to help me guess what it could be. Finally on returning home and entering the house, I found two lovely pictures on the piano. One was a painting of Mt. Hood taken from the Dalles, done by Miss Mary Bridges, and the other was a painting representing a man's hand, handing a bunch of pansies to a lady's hand. The gift of these kind friends was an entire surprise as neither of us had heard a word about it before."

On January 6, Will preached the New Year's sermon on the text found in the ninth verse of the Ninetieth Psalm, "We spend our years as a tale that is told."

Janette's Diary says:

January 8, 1884.

"According to appointment a church meeting was held in Turner Jan. 8th. Meeting opened by singing, scripture reading and prayer by Will. After remarks by him on object of meeting, it was moved by Elder S. Condit that we proceed to take measures to organize a Presbyterian Church in Turner. After free discussion, the motion was put and carried unanimously by standing vote. It was moved and seconded that Will circulate paper of membership and that March 1st be the day of organizing ... The week of prayer was kept here at Turner, it had never been observed before and was quite well attended, even better than at Salem. Our smallest attendance being 28, theirs 16. At each meeting Will made a short talk on topic for the evening and called on some one for prayer and on people for a verse of Scripture. Then too we had singing."

When the rainy season came Janette had said, "It is no wonder that they call the people of Oregon 'webfoot'." It rained day after day and when it did not rain it was dull, foggy and misty and that was even more disagreeable than the rain. In spite of the wood stoves the house always felt damp. Janette's cough came back and the housework tired her, but she never gave up or complained. She did her best to keep cheerful for Will's sake. When he asked her anxiously how she was, she replied, "Well, I almost fell into the slough of despond today, but with patience and courage I continued my journey."

Besides the housework and cooking there were always guests to entertain, calls to make and meetings to attend. By the end of the day, Janette cared only to lie on the couch in the study while Will read to her whenever he had the time. But her Diary shows that she kept on with her church work. She always found time to help anyone who needed her. Many found it an inspiration just to visit with her. Her cheerful manner was contagious. She had a way of seeing the funny side of things, as her Diary tells. Yet she had sympathy for all, the sick and the sorrowing, and she was interested in anything that concerned her friends. It is no wonder that she was so greatly loved.

From Janette's Diary of Friday, January 25:

"Will went to Aurora to attend the funeral of Mrs. Gribble. He took the 6 A.M. train thirty-five miles to Aurora, then rode a cayuse pony seven miles to the house and preached the sermon which called for the expression of deep sympathy. The funeral procession consisted of six two-horse wagons. They proceeded to a lonely fir forest where in the heart of it was a clearing of about seventy-five yards square. This was the cemetery fenced around with a snake fence of logs. It was a dull, drizzly, sleety day. A fire was built nearby so that the family and friends might warm themselves. The whole scene was weird and lonely, a desolate place to think of leaving a dear one ... Then Will had the long ride on the pony back to the depot and home on the evening train. The poor, dear, tired fellow was a long time recovering from the effect of such a trip."

From Janette's Diary, February 18:

"Last Wednesday at our Missionary Society Mrs. Hilleary read an interesting essay and had a motion before Society which was carried to have Will deliver a lecture for us on: 'Girls.' Will joked over the matter said he would not do it, 'nothing in the subject.' On Saturday, a long article in Daily States-man said, 'Rev. Mr. Young when asked to deliver lecture on girls, their influence and education, refused to do it saying it was not worth it.' We judge the author to be Mrs. Cornelius and people say she is a strong woman's rights woman.

"Mr. Hill delivered a very interesting lecture before about eighty people in the interest of our Society. Subject: Alaska, he had with him a number of curiosities from Alaska.

"Up to Sat. night we had 11 in. snow. I coaxed Will to write he would not be at Marion which he did. But being communion at Pleasant Grove he felt he must go there. None had been in from that neighborhood on account of slough, but that day several came to Turner to preparatory service, said they drove right over slough on the ice. About 5 o'clock we started in the buggy to Condits, got to Cyreneus about dusk, had to go across fields from there following a horse track in the snow. Will had to get out and walk part of way follow-ing it. But we got there safely, had a pleasant evening. Next morning followed their sled to Pleasant Grove Church. There were by this time 16 inches of snow. However about 30 were present. It was a memorable service for Will. For the first time he administered the ordinance of baptism. He baptized eight and received three into membership ... Mrs. Neal said that the first thing that convinced her baptism of children was right was Hannah consecrating Samuel.

"We took dinner at Neals', started home about 3 in a blind-ing snowstorm, had to let the horse walk all the way till within a mile of Turner but soon the sun came out and the ride was not so disagreeable."

After that Janette's cough was worse and she had to stay in the house for a few days but she put aside her own feelings to prepare for the Literary Program. They decided to have a Literary and

Basket Sociable in Blakeney Hall to raise money to put in a board walk up to the church. As Janette told the Committee:

"The condition is really disgraceful. Even with rubbers and gossamers, the ladies can hardly get across the sea of mud and must hold their skirts up off the ground. You know that it is really very undignified for the minister to arrive at the church in high muddy boots and have to carry in his wife as Will did last Sunday."

She wrote of this program in her Diary February 24:

"The program was as follows:

Instrumental Duet—Miss Bridges and Miss Ethel Cummings

Reading, 'Betsey and I are out,'—Mrs. McKinney

Song by Glee Club—'The Chase'

Reading—'How Betsey and I made up'—Mrs. Cromwell

Song by Glee Club—'Greeting Glee'

Vocal Duet, 'Angel Meet Me at the crossroads,' sung by Mr. and Mrs. Young.

Recitation by Etta Hilleary, 'Ride of Jennie McNeal'

Quartette—Mr. McKinney, Mr. Dunbar, Mr. Robinson, and Mr. Young.

"I did all the playing and it was miserable enough. After this 'monopoly' as Will expressed it the numbers and corresponding names were read off, each gentleman claimed his number of basket and hunted up his lady named. Will bought two baskets, one sent in by Alice Smith, who was not present with us, but at a dance, so he ate with Mrs. O.H.P. Cornelius, I with Mr. John Blakney's son Louie. After a pleasant social time, we left at 10 o'clock. In the meantime an opposition party had obtained access to Mr. Cromwell's dance house and were having their good time. Mrs. Cornelius told me about the intention of some to have entertainment and dance too, though knowing Will's opposition. We were much hurt and worried over it, but we trust good will yet result. The result financially was $20—$3 of which goes to pay for the hall. 'Tis said (after all the ado made by the Cromwells) that $8 was raised by the dancers expecting they would have to pay for the hall. Mr. Cromwell did not charge them so they gave it to the board walk fund."

VI. Oregon Circuit Rider

More than fifty years later, at a meeting in Will's honor held on January 21, 1935, Dr. Guy W. Wadsworth, retired President of Occidental College, said:

"We people who build beautiful highways don't remember what it meant to ride in a buggy with a patient horse—more or less patient —over those rough roads in Oregon. He was a circuit rider, and it was a mighty good thing for him to start his ministry in this way."

While living in Turner Will's pastorate included Gervais, Woodburn, Pleasant Grove and Marion. So he was serving an area of about 25 miles radius from his home. Many of the entries in Janette's Diary have to do with the pastoral calls that they made, trying to interest the people in organizing Sunday Schools and churches. It seems that most of those to whom they talked made excuses. Some wanted a Sunday School for their children but didn't want to attend church themselves. One man refused to be an elder because he couldn't control his temper. Another said he had known so many ministers who were frauds that his faith was shaken. Nearly all the farmers used the excuse of Sunday work. When the sun shone they had to take advantage of it. All this would have discouraged any man less consecrated than Will and less sure of his calling.

While still in the Seminary, he had heard Dr. Thomas Fraser make a strong appeal for men to come to the coast where the fields were open and ripe for harvest. Years later Will wrote:

"I shall never forget the opening sentences of his address. They ran about like this: 'I come to you as a Synodical missionary of a territory that is bounded on the East by the Rocky Mountains, on the South by the country of Mexico, on the West by the Pacific Ocean and on the North by the Aurora Borealis'."

His acceptance of that call, and his devotion to it, showed the ruling motive of his whole life: to serve God and man.

The Diary also tells of the many visits to the neighboring towns to hold protracted meetings. Janette accompanied him whenever possible. While Will could stand the hard drives through rain and mud and over corduroy roads, he would be worn after the long drives. But in his eagerness to spread the gospel, he did not think of himself. But Janette sometimes wrote of being very tired by these drives.

When bad weather set in, Will found it more and more difficult to drive out to Woodburn, Gervais, Pleasant Grove and Marion. He was pleased when Presbytery decided to give up Woodburn, and to organize a church at Turner with some members from the mother church of Pleasant Grove. The people at Turner had wanted a church there for some time. But Will did not want to do anything that would detract from Pleasant Grove and hurt the Condits' feelings, since their family had such a long connection with that church. Will spoke to the Condits very tactfully, and it was pleasantly agreed. The new church was called "Octorara Church," at Will's suggestion. Thus it was named for the old church at Parkesburg, Pennsylvania, founded in 1720 when that land was still a home for Indians and an almost unbroken wilderness. Will's ancestor, Arthur Parke, and his wife, Mary, had been charter members.

Janette wrote:

March 5.

"Last Sunday [March 2] was an eventful day for us, for it witnessed the establishing of a Presbyterian Church in Turner. The week previous Will spent in preparing a carefully written sermon on Gen. XVII. 7. 'The Abrahamic Covenant' ... The sermon was full of Scriptural doctrine suited to the occasion and after it Will read a brief history of Pleasant Grove Church as follows:

'On the 25th of Sept. 1856 at 1 o'clock P.M. the first meeting in regard to the organization of Pleasant Grove was held. It organized with 9 members, 8 only of whom are living today. Then the record, after describing the different meetings concludes—

'Thus another little vine is planted in this desert. We trust it is a vine of God's own planting. May His richest blessing rest upon it and may it bring forth much fruit that His name may be glorified. This prayer has been answered. This vine has grown and strengthened, has had 71 members 10 of whom have died, 18 been dismissed leaving 43 on the roll today ...

'Humbly confessing submission to Almighty God, gratefully acknowledging our debt to Him and sincerely expressing our desire to walk together in truth and love as members of His visible church on earth, the better to prepare ourselves by His blessing for the service of the invisible church in heaven.

'Resolved that we adopt the confession of faith of the General Assembly of the Presbyterian Church of U.S. as our rule of faith and plan of government and discipline.

'Resolved that this church be named 'Octorara.'

'Resolved that the petition as signed be carried to the meeting of Presbytery in conference at Eugene City the 18th of this month for their approval...'

"The whole service was impressive. Mrs. Hilleary said afterward that even Mr. Young was more earnest than usual. Since Pleasant Grove is five miles out in the country and Turner is a village of more than twenty eight houses it seemed wiser to have the church at Turner.

"The Octorara Church was organized with 18 members and 2 more have since united. Will wrote immediately to Mr. Marshall, the pastor of the Upper Octorara Church at Parkesburg asking that they present the new church with a communion set."

Janette writes:
March 26.

"Letter came from Mr. Marshall saying if we could get along this time by next time he would endeavor to have a communion service for us from Octorara Church."

Janette tells of going to Eugene for the meeting of Presbytery:
March 26.

"I went on 11 o'clock train, glad that I was on my way to meet Will, who had been away since Tuesday 11th. He went to Wilbur preached there Tuesday night, was annoyed by five fellows talking. After sermon Mr. L. got up and thanked the audience for their kind attention, which the audience no doubt took as a bit of cool sarcasm. After service they rode two miles, stayed all night, slept in a narrow bed. Will took cold. Rode next morning to Oakland 7 miles in a two-horse wagon. Preached at Oakland Wednesday and Thursday nights and during day made calls. Will disgusted because L. talked so much about the girls. Rev. Lee came and preached Friday and Saturday night and Sunday A.M. and Will Sunday night and deep earnestness pervaded the meetings, some fifteen confessed Christ. Sunday afternoon a family came around to call on them. The parents were Christians but children and all were ready to unite with the church. Monday Will came on to Prairies preached there and Tuesday met me at Eugene City. But poor fellow he was so sick and weak he could hardly walk and as soon as we got to our stopping place, Mrs. Osborn's he lay down until eve. His continued work preaching and riding in rough wagons and at Prairies walking two miles on R.R. tracks after service in night air had brought on an attack of vertigo and a sleepless night and a sick day. But he insisted on going to Presbytery in eve and next morn was himself again for which I was very grateful.

"The meetings of Presbytery were very interesting. There seems to be harmony among the Brethren. Mr. E. T. Lockhard and W. O. Fobes were ordained. The most impressive meeting to Will was the one in regard to salary. He saw as never before how men will deny themselves to preach the gospel. How meager their salaries, how hard they work. Mr. Wadhams said, 'Why these self-sacrificing, intelligent men get not as much as one of my truck men who require no brains for their work. It is a shame.'

"We ladies walked to the top of Skinner's butte overlooking the city. The warm sunlight, the wild flowers, the extended view all combined to make us very happy."

Soon it was spring and the robins came back. The first thing to bloom was the red flowering currant that puts forth flowers before leaves. There were several varieties, shading from pale rose to crimson, the flowers arranged in clusters on a slender stem and very graceful. The came the blossoms on the wild fruit trees, plum and cherry, and the wild flowers, the California poppies, blue lupins, Indian paint brushes, and buttercups, until the fields looked like beautiful Persian carpets. New leaves came out on the trees and bulbs came up in Janette's garden.

All this gave Easter a new meaning for her. She taught her class of girls the Easter song, "Christ the Lord is Risen Today." They helped her decorate the church with sprays of white lilies and she was pleased when several of them united with the church on Easter Sunday. Will chose the text for his sermon from the sixth verse of the twentieth chapter of Matthew, "He is not here for He is risen as He said."

When Janette came home from the Missionary Society, Will asked her if they had had a good meeting.

"Oh, yes, they liked my talk on the Umatilla Indians. Cassie Cole played the piano for Mary Cairns to sing 'The Indian Girl's Lament'."

"Mrs. Condit made the cake that was served with the tea, but I could have baked a better one. Oh, yes, do you remember that girl you married last fall? I think her name was Mary Denyer. Now she is Mrs. Smith. Well, she is in the family way. Mrs. Cornelius' daughter is going with that nice young man, Ed. Squires, who sings in our choir. She hopes it will be a match. Poor Grandma Robinson is sick with typhoid fever. Mrs. Rutherford likes to hear you preach because you don't read your sermons. Mrs. Atkinson wants to see you about having her baby baptized but they can't decide upon a name. I asked her why she didn't name him for you."

Will laughingly asked, "Who is gossiping now?"

"Why Will, you ought to be ashamed of yourself. I wasn't gossiping, I was only giving you the news of friends."

Janette writes of good news in her Diary:

April 8.

"We were happy to receive a letter from Annie and Hervey Dickey telling of the arrival of a little daughter, Laura. We rejoiced with them. In congratulating them Will addressed: Miss Laura Snead Dickey, Livermore, Iowa.

'My dear Laura.

'Welcome to the world of light and fight. Soon you will learn This world is the best you will live in, to lend or to spend or to give in. But to beg or to borrow or to get your own, it's the very worst world that ever was known. You will have to struggle and strain for a hearing often, but the more noise you can make the more attention you can attract . . . You will have to sit before you creep and creep before you walk and fall down many times before you can stand alone . . . You will be fondled a good deal partly on your own account and partly on the account of those nearest of kin. Be patient under it all. We are to bear one another's burdens in this life . . . When by chance a pin runs through too far and pricks, cry loud and long, not only until you are picked up, but also until the difficulties are set right... Don't be too good, lest you die young and furnish a heroine for a Sunday School book. Heroines are becoming scarce. Never allow anyone to gull or guzzle you.

'With much love to you and kind regards to your parents, I am very sincerely and affectionately your friend, W.S. Young.

'P.S. Please keep it a secret, but I would like to bespeak your heart and hand for my oldest boy. Of course this in the future but keep it quiet until the day arrives. W.S.Y.'"
April 8.

"The Salem church called Rev. E. J. Thompson and his son-in-law Mr. Pritchard came with him... Will meeting him by chance in Salem discovered that he knew him two years ago in Union Seminary. Will suggested the Woodburn field to him and wrote immediately to Mr. Condit. Mr. C. had already thought of such a plan. They all know Will has too much work and needs the time to devote to this field. I shall be glad to have him released from that and hope that he will not plan more work here that will require an undue amount of riding. He now has another service at Pleasant Grove on afternoon of 4th sabbath—has decided to postpone building and organizing at Marion till Fall.

"In a recent sermon of Mr. Vanscoy on 'I had rather be a door-keeper' etc., he gave as an illustration a case of an old man who was sexton of a church who swept and lit the lamps. Who, though humble, lifted his voice in praise with the rich in the church and ended pathetically 'but the old man is gone where there will be no more lighting of coal oil.'

"On the 10th of April we attended the Institute at Albany. Will having been invited by Prof. E. B. McElroy, State Superintendent, to lecture on 'Use and Abuse of the English Language.' Will worked hard at it and found the pleasure of writing good drill for him. We went up Thursday morning, were met and escorted by Mr. Condit to his home where we were kindly entertained. Find his wife improves on acquaintance. He is very helpful to her about the housework as she is not strong. In the afternoon we went to the Courthouse, and the room I shall not forget. On the wide platform, sat at one table five young ladies, committee on names and instead of registering as we are accustomed to, these ladies were to hunt the teachers up and solicit their names. At another table sat several men, reporters with maps, blackboards and everything betokening a vast amount of work done and to be done. In the body of the room was an audience that at first glance was not as refined looking as one would have expected. Still there were many prominent men and good critics present. Prof. Wychoff of Albany University gave an interesting lecture on Hygiene, which consumed so much time that it was time to adjourn ere Will was called on. A few who had work to do left, but the audience gave marked attention considering they had been seated so long. One place in his lecture Will spoke of the class of men who think they are capable of editing a newspaper. It appeared like a joke to many who had in mind just such an editor in town.

"The Albany Herald in writing of Will's talk, said that he was listened to 'with eagerness notwithstanding the audience had been seated for over three hours and the very close attention given him was complimentary to his ability as an essayist.'

"In the evening instead of having one good first class lecture, three different men lectured and from the mispronunciations it seemed like a parody to hear such at a Teacher's Institute.

"We got our visit to Condits at last and Mrs. Condit took us to call on Mrs. Peck whose husband drinks so — but she attends Pleasant Grove, sometimes having to walk as far to get a horse in the field as she would to walk to church. Her grandmother a good old Welsh lady lives with her part of the time, we did not meet her but saw her Welsh bible. Mrs. Peck showed Will her letter from her pastor in Kansas dismissing them to another church. She spoke of the church privileges she had had in Kansas and said her happiest time was when at Pleasant Grove. She apologized to Mrs. Condit for being in the kitchen but said she liked it there. 'The walls seem like friends.' They were near to her.

"Last Monday Mr. Adams' father was buried from here. Will attended the funeral but had no part—sat back and took in all the strange services. The hymns were most odd. The minister lined them and not being ones the people knew he had to sing them also and while the friends took a last took at the corpse one minister stood near and with closed eyes drawled, 'Oh for a closer walk with Thee.' The sermon was by a hard shell Baptist. The text being several verses he literally when persecuted in one verse fled on to the next and quoted irrelevant passages and commented on the same from Genesis to Revelations. His assistant wore no collar and had dirty clothes on.

"Our Missionary Society sent a box to Mrs. Arndt in South Dakota, on which Will paid the freight $5.25 and made me promise I would not tell. The box contained a bonnet, two dress patterns, 25 yards muslin, a sheet, a tablecloth, 4 yards calico, buttons, five pairs stockings and two comforts."

Janette's Diary continues:

May 5.

"Our little home looks neater and more inviting than ever to us for we have been painting and cleaning. The parlor is dressed in white and the yellow doors will soon be forgotten. Our room has a neat blue paper. On Sunday there was solid satisfaction in sitting down and taking a survey of it all. Will got a neat frame that just matches the grey and gilt in our marriage certificate and now it hangs on the wall.

"The ceiling had been whitewashed and we wanted it papered, of course it had to be cheese clothed first. Will and Mr. Kaufman had a serious time getting the muslin tacked on. They stretched their arms and necks and got dust in their eyes and when it was done — decided it looked well enough without papering. I wanted to have the stove moved into the woodshed but Will said it would take double the insurance so one day he surprised me with a coal-oil stove large enough to cook several things at one time and with a nice oven. Then the next eve as I went into the pantry I saw the dearest little victual's safe. That I guessed immediately had been made for our pantry and true when Will confessed — he had ordered it in Salem and got it quietly home as a surprise for me. But these are only a few of the many kind helpful things he gets and does for me."

Janette tells of their first wedding anniversary:

"On the ninth day of May we received a crimson pincushion worked in Kensington stitch from Fannie and Clara and an emery bag from Mother. This note was attached: 'Dear

Brother and Sister. — A small token of remembrance of your wedding anniversary.'

"Receiving it on Friday and coming so unexpectedly we appreciated it very much."

It was a beautiful day. Since their wedding anniversary came on Sunday, Janette put up a basket lunch and they went out into the woods for a picnic. Will made a great pile of bracken ferns on which she could recline and they talked of their happy year together and how God had blessed them. The next day they had a pleasant ride to Woodburn. Along the roadside they saw buttercups, daisies and columbine. Through the trees one could see the white blossoms of the dogwood. Fruit trees were in bloom and looked like big white bouquets. The wrote of their stay in Woodburn:

May 12.

"It was a pleasure to be with Will. On the 11th we went to S.S. The Superintendent came and asked me to take charge of the young ladies Bible class. I could not refuse. I saw a twinkle in Will's eye though, and he confessed afterwards that he had sent the Superintendent to me.

"We learned that Mr. Kean the Cumberland Presbyterian preacher had the Sunday before preached such an interesting and so entirely different a sermon than usual that the people remarked about it. Then he learned that Mr. K. had been visiting Turner and had heard Will's children's sermon on the same subject. And to crown all, Will found the outline of his sermon in the pulpit bible. We all had a good laugh over it.

"The 25th of May Will was at Brownsville by appointment of committee at Presbytery to preach on 'Giving.' He saw no one at the train to meet him, so sat on the depot porch till late in the afternoon when Mr. Templeton drove in and took him home, small house, large family. Will slept in room with two others, 10 persons in a house no larger than Sam Jackson's [A very small stone house on the Parkesburg farm].

"Sunday Will gave a brief talk to the S.S. then preached at Church service, no organ, a leader who ran the scale and pitched the tune and when the tune was ended looked up at Will and nodded as much as to say, 'We are through, now you go on.' In afternoon preached children's sermon in Methodist S.S. by request and later another sermon in the Presbyterian

Church. It was a full tiresome day. Mr. Templeton on being asked by Will if his sermon seemed long, 'not more than thirty minutes.' It really had been fifty minutes. He said that he hadn't intended it to be so long, but he hadn't noticed any sleepy heads. 'No,' said Mr. T. 'When we have a new man we keep awake to watch him. We know not what kind of pranks he may cut up—but our pastor, good old man! been with us so many years we know all will go on all right so we can sleep without compunction.'

"Will took dinner with Mrs. Martha Beamer, a pious widow lady. She promised him if he builds a church she will help, having no relatives to leave her money to.

"At Woodburn a few Sundays ago a woman walked five miles to hear the Methodist minister. When church was over she said to him, 'Well, if I had known you were going to read your sermon I would have stayed at home. I have better sermons at home I could have read.'"
June 30.

"Saturday morning, Will had gone for bean poles. I was dishwashing when the door bell rang. I found a stranger at the door who wanted to see Mr. Y. I said not at home but would be ere long. He declined to wait. It wasn't long until he called again. Will had returned so I sent him to the barn wondering to myself if he wanted to buy Prince, thinking that quite likely. I immediately began giving reasons why we didn't want to part with him. My fears were soon quieted by Will coming in with a grin saying that Mr. Albert M. Mulhey wished to marry Bertha Paynes of Mehama, failing to get an Episcopalian minister he came to Will. Will consented. About eleven o'clock we left for Mehama but had a hard time finding it. The men at the store suggested we go two miles out of town to the Cox's. So on we went up the hills, found the place were met at the door by a quiet lady who did not say stay, but Will began removing his duster. Whereupon she asked me to take off my wraps. Will explained how we came, it seemed all right. She soon excused herself and we entertained ourselves. They have a large family and are noted for having more company than anyone around . . . The parlor was papered with dark blue calico it looked neat. The sitting room was papered with newspapers and had yellow muslin curtains edged with black lace. On the wall hung on two pairs of antlers, were three rifles, a seven shooter and a pistol and a cougar skin on the floor.

"The table was bountifully spread. They expected us to help ourselves. The bread was hot biscuit. During dinner I picked a hair out of the butter and Mr. Cox took one from Will's plate. Will remarked, 'It is just one of my whiskers.' The milk looked rich and I think was clean.

"In commenting later on the dinner Will said, 'Good enough what there was of it and enough of it unless it was better'." The Diary continues:

"Our room was about the size, or perhaps smaller than the room at Condit's. The bed of wool, (lumpy) the pillows, a mere name. Will doubled his coat and used it. There was neither comb, brush or other necessaries. The cracks in the door and ceiling were large enough to see through. The curtain was a very dirty white one. The carpet was one small rug.

"Saturday in the school house nearby that afternoon there was an audience of twenty six, service was over before dark. We met one woman, a Pennsylvanian, Mrs. B., who with her two boys climbed fences and came through fields to get there. She had on a wrapper and sunbonnet, but next morning was neatly dressed in black. Sunday morning at Mehama there was a congregation of 45 in the school house, the singing was good, an old melodeon of Dr. Pratt's was used. The people were earnest, attentive listeners. Beside me sat a pretty young lady dressed in a gay lawn. After service, I asked her if she lived near. 'I am a sister of the bride where you go today.'

"No one asking us to dinner we hurried off to be there at one o'clock. We drove past Cox's and soon after began the ascent of the mountain. First four miles of corduroy, (rails laid crosswise close together in the road.) This is a kind of road quite common in Oregon. Then on till we met a man who told us that most folks left their teams at the foot of the mountain and walked up, but there was a rough wagon road if we chose to take it.

"Not wishing to walk we started to drive up, but ere we got half way wished we had left the team at the foot. The trees were so close to the track that we lowered the top of the buggy and fortunate it was for soon we came to a narrow place with a tree on one side and a steep grade on the other. It was too narrow to turn around, so Will whipped up the horse but about half way across the wheels struck a stone throwing them off the ground on one side. There we balanced for a few seconds, but Will's presence of mind led him to draw Prince around and soon we were safely over and free to breathe. The groom had come down to meet us so piloted us up the rest of the steep grade. The folks at the house as soon as they saw that we had started up the hill, trembled for us. It would have been too hazardous for us to attempt to descend that way for our buggy had no brake, but we were shown out another way which was better."

Despite the poor road they enjoyed the beauty of the rhododendrons with their purple blossoms, the pink and white blossoms of the mountain laurel and the wild lilacs. When they got to the top they found it was quite level around the house, with a hill in the background. The view of the surrounding hills and across to Fox Valley was lovely and they feasted their eyes while the horse was being attended to.

Janette's description continues:

"The groom took us in, and we were met at the door by the bride's mother, Mrs. Snyder, who to our surprise was stylishly dressed in black silk. On entering we found that the home showed evidences of refinement. After a delay of about an hour the groom went to the room after the bride, but she was not ready. He walked over and sat down in a corner. Soon she appeared, looked around a moment for him, he did not see her so without any more ado she walked past him saying, 'Come on Albert' took her place by the window. He saw and followed. Will likewise. There was a hurrying in of the guests and Will proceeded with the Episcopal ceremony as requested. The only blunder being the groom saying, 'Shall I repeat after you this?' At its close some ladies sang 'Blest be the tie that binds.' Then Will and I had lunch and started off riding all the way home that night tired and sore from riding over rough roads. Monday we rested and entertained callers getting by mail a letter from Mr. Voorhees asking if Will could help him obtain work for a young man who wanted to come west and make his way, will come highly recommended. Will and Mr. Crawford said to Mr. V. 'Tell him to come on. Hands will be needed on farms!'"

July 2.

"Wednesday. People are flocking past here in teams and wagons holding six to eight on their way to Salem to attend Cole's circus. It seems amusing to us. The people complain of money being scarce but there will be plenty spent today.

"On Monday June 23, we drove to Woodburn, stayed overnight talked up the plan of organizing a church at Gervais. Tuesday night spent at Hardings, five miles from Gervais. Mrs. H. is a daughter of the Osborns in Eugene, and is a member of the Presbyterian Church there. We had a pleasant visit, slept upstairs! brussels carpet in the room! Next morning got some yellow pond lilies drove home 35 miles, was in the wagon from 8:30 a.m. till 4 p.m. Good road, stood the ride well."

July 15.

"On Thursday July 10th we both went to Gervais, took tea at Dr. Cauthorn's. We drove to Percy's where we stayed over night. Mrs. P. will go into the organization. They are Episcopalians he is an Englishman, has been in Australia, finally settled in Kansas. On account of his wife's health came to Oregon. They have been accustomed to help their minister as shown from Mr. P. saying if Will was near enough he would haul him a load of hay. When time for worship the mother asked which she should get the prayer book or the bible? We were put to sleep in a small room scantily furnished the bed a feather one which had probably been brought from Kansas where bed bugs are plentiful, for I scratched and Will scratched and in the room beside ours as I lay awake in the darkness, I could distinctly hear the little girl give an angry whine and a vicious scratch. In the morning in making the bed I found four bed bugs and one flea.

"It being Will's birthday on July 11, 1884 [he was 25 years old] I slipped a little box out where he could see it. When he opened it, he found that it contained a pair of shirt studs made from my hair. He was completely surprised not having had an inkling of it, though knowing that I was sending for a gold pen for him.

"We went from place to place trying to get people to promise to go into the organization. Several gave their names.

At last we went back to Mr. Voorhees getting there after nearly all had retired.   He called us 'Night Owls.'

"After a good night's rest in a big room and big feather bed, we spent Saturday resting and talking to Mrs. Voorhees and Mollie just back from California.   Will went to Gervais. Met Mr. Evan Pritchard at the train and brought him over to the Voorhees where we spent a pleasant evening.   Sunday we attended church in Woodburn and S.S.

"Mr. John Vandever has the bible class now and makes a good teacher.   He is a worthy man and faithful bible student.   Mr. Pritchard preached so Will got a rest for the first time since coming to Oregon a year ago.

"In the afternoon we went to Gervais and met the Rev. R. W. Hill and Elder John Crawford there.   After a sermon by Mr. Pritchard from Exodus XIV, 15, 'Speak unto the children of Israel that they go forward,' the congregation was led in prayer for the divine blessing on what was about to be done. Then Will read the following signed petition.   'We the undersigned members or applicants for membership do respectfully petition the presbytery of Oregon for their approval of the organization of the Presbyterian Church of Gervais, Oregon' ... This was signed by fourteen members.   Mr. Voorhees was duly installed elder in accordance with the wishes of the people.

"The Reverend Robert W. Hill then pronounced the Presbyterian Church of Gervais duly organized and proceeded to administer the Communion emphasizing the thought that the wine was not Christ's blood but the symbol and the bread was not Christ's body but the symbol.   Thus another center for good in a needy community is started."

This they thought was especially important, since fully half of the town and community was made up of Roman Catholics and they had a large church and convent there.   There was no other Christian Church in this center.   Will had been preaching once a month for a year, but now the Reverend Evan R. Pritchard took charge of the work.

Three weeks later Will wrote:

August 2.

"On getting my mail got a letter in mourning envelope — but thought it was to Janette from Josie Mink, so paid no attention to it.   Stopped at the barn and then came on home.

On seeing it was not for Janette, she opened it and read, 'Yourself and family are kindly invited to attend the funeral of Rev. H. S. Dickey from the residence of his uncle J. Hamilton Ross on Thursday, July 3rd, 1884 at 10 o'clock. Internment at Fogg's Manor.' How it shocked us. We were expecting daily a letter from him. Did not know definitely he was home. Did not know he was seriously sick or sick at all. So sad! so confusing to human thought. How lonesome it made me feel. How unsatisfactory such a notice! How much farther away we seemed from our own dear ones. We tried to write to Annie and each did but it was so hard and the pages penned could have been written with tears. I had lost from earth more than a friend and classmate, I had lost a tried and true brother one whom I had learned to love for his own true worth. Two years we roomed together at college and after he visited me at Union. Then poor lonely Annie and her little baby. How undeserving kind seemed God to us! But the past we could not keep from our minds. Annie's letter since received tells all the particulars... The Psalms read were Hervey's favorite ones, 23rd and 37th and the hymn 'Nearer My God to Thee' was by request. The funeral was very large."

Hervey was 30 years old, just at the beginning of a promising ministry. Janette deeply sympathized with Will, for Hervey was her dear friend also. They prayed that God would support Annie in this her hour of deepest trouble and would comfort their sorrowing hearts. Sharing their sorrow seemed to bring them closer together in their love for each other. They thought back to their wedding day when they were all so happy together. Then a few days later they were at Annie's and Hervey's wedding. They had the memory of those happy days to comfort them. In writing about the service for Hervey, Janette admitted that she didn't like the last verse of "Nearer My God to Thee":

> "Or if on joyful wing
> Cleaving the sky
> Sun, moon and stars forgot
> Upward I fly."

It made heaven seem so far away. She said she would rather think of it as being close at hand than up among the stars.

VII. *Pleasing Prospects*

Wanting to see more of Oregon, Will and Janette took a camping trip through the great forests of the Coast Range to the shores of the Pacific. These interesting experiences Janette describes in her Diary. She gives no dates except Monday, August 4, the day they started, and Thursday, August 21, when they returned.

August 21.

"We returned today from our trip to Coos Bay, had a delightful time but must begin my story back at August 4. Monday morning, we hurried around doing the work, cooking chicken for lunch on trip, had Blakeneys here cleaning the well got dressed and ready for train by dint of hurry and worry. Had a ride of 121 miles on cars to Oakland, got there at six in the evening, rested and stayed all night at James Young's. Nice cordial people, Mr. Lockhard's standby. Next morning started about eight in a two horse wagon, four springs, no top but easy to ride."

Mr. Lockhard made all the arrangements and accompanied them. They felt very gay and care free. Summer was at its height and the pleasant weather made their trip very enjoyable. Janette was glad that, back in Pennsylvania, she had encouraged her pupils to bring her wild flowers, which she had tried to identify. Some of the Oregon flowers were familiar but others were new to her. Along the road beside the snake fences of logs grew buttercups, black-eyed susans, tall two foot stands of blue lupins, and thickets of wild roses.

When they neared Booth's Ferry to cross the Umpqua river, the pastures were full of daisies, lambs' tongue, and big stands of iris. There were patches of sky blue camas, the star shaped Oregon lily whose roots the Indians used to make bread. Many plants had Indian names and were connected with Indian legends and ceremonies. In the forest itself there were not so many flowering plants, but the ground and fallen trees were covered with a luxurious carpet of moss and ferns. The fields of wheat and oats stood almost knee high. By this time they had gotten used to the ugly blackened stumps of trees in the fields. In the meadows scampered playful lambs, who ran up to peep at them through the logs of the fences.

The Diary continues:

"About noon we came to Booth's Ferry — steep sides to bank — called to a ferryman to ferry us over. He had to dip a quantity of water out of his boat ere he could come across. Mr. L. got tired waiting. He said he could do it himself and save fifty cents. I was too timid to trust him. Will knew it so insisted on having ferryman. We got across nicely and paid the man twenty-five cents...

"We went on several miles until we came to a house on one of the beautiful oak covered hills where we stopped to lunch. The horses seemed about used up, Mr. Lockhard's horse being young and unused to travel. While camping there, an old blind man came out of the house and learning that we were going to Coos, had much to tell us about the road and the people. While there I found a moss agate. The country through there is beautiful. The oak forests look so homelike to me after seeing only fir trees for a year.

"We drove through oak groves and open country till dark. Soon we struck fir timber and we thought we must be near the 10 mile house at the foot of the mountain, but it was a saw-mill and the houses there were not inviting for at one the pigs were under and on the porches — so we hurried on. It being then dusk we had a long lonely hill to climb and after riding up and up for over an hour we came to a house but rejoiced too soon, for they told us to go on further. Between 8 and 9 we came to 18 mile house."

In Oregon, as Will wrote in one of his letters to the *Chester Valley Union,* "Every house was a public house." So the men put on their ministerial dignity and Will called out, "Madame, can we spend the night with you?" The housewife, Mrs. Brown, was very kind and they had comfortable beds and a good night's sleep. For breakfast the next morning they had fawn, hot square sour-dough biscuit fresh from the oven, stewed apples, blackberry jam, coffee and a big jug of milk. They rarely saw eggs, although there were plenty of hens.

Again Janette tells of the trip:

"In the morning about seven we left. Soon came to the toll gate, paid $1.50 for team, went on, soon came to nineteen mile house. Then we began the ascent of the Coast range in earnest. Up we went winding around for four or five miles until we reached the top, the very top.

"We could distinguish it because the ridge was quite narrow. There was a space of cleared land too, as if an attempt had been made at settlement. Then we began the descent which was more gradual. We travelled on till dark when we came to what we thought was our stopping place, but seeing big pigs going in the back door and little ones going in the front door, decided us to drive on rapidly. After going up, up, until the old moon peeped through the timber at us and the miles seemed long we emerged into an open space. On seeing a house, we shouted, 'Beds for two?' 'What place is this?' We soon learned that this was the place to stay. When bedtime came the hostess came in and looked at us. Seeing Will and I sitting near together she said, 'Is one of you man and wife?'

"It was so dark that they could not see to put the horses away. They took a candle up into the hay mow and set it on a log. Great quantities of chittin wood are gotten in this neighborhood. They just take the bark and get nine dollars an cwt. It is used as a medicine, a little of the bark acts as a cathartic."

The Spanish padres learned to appreciate that wood, and named it "cascara sagrada" or sacred bark.

The Diary goes on to say:

"The house was built of split cedar logs, some windowless rooms and as full of people as a beehive. The chimney was built of sticks and dirt as children build a pen of corn cobs. Our room was partitioned off from the kitchen and had no ceiling in it. There was a cold draft from the garret. We had a wash bowl and pitcher, but Mr. Lockhard had to go out on the porch to get to his room and had to go out of doors to wash.

"For breakfast we had hot bread, potatoes, rice, bacon and honey. I guess things were clean. When the bread plate was empty the father called to his daughter, 'Missourie here'."

The next morning they went on to Sumner, travelling through a timbered region. Here and there were open plots, small clearings that showed that somebody had tried to live there and raise a little crop of oats and wheat and had failed. There were a number of deserted log cabins chinked with mud. The roof poles had rotted and the roofs fallen in. The land was overgrown with thistles, and all looked very desolate.

Janette wrote:

"'Twas even more lonely to us than the mountains, for there we were not expecting people to live. We passed the 'True half-way house,' and rode through miles and miles of myrtle-wood groves. The wood admits of high polish and is beautifully grained. We saw tables and ornaments made of it. [That wood, besides being native to Oregon, is also found in the Holy Land.]

"Reaching Sumner we were introduced to Rev. Mr. Bailey, Baptist minister who kindly promised to get our horses in pasture there, so we got a man to drive us to Coos City and take the team back to Sumner."

On the way they went through a section where logging was going on. The lumberjacks were felling huge Douglas firs 300 feet tall, using two-handed saws. The timber was hauled to the lumber mills to be sawed into boards. Only the big and choice logs found their way to the mills. Other logs, that it would not pay to haul, were left on the forest floor to be burned along with the "slash."

As Janette describes it:

"We saw a tramway (with logs embedded in the ground much like the ties of a railway track though not so close,) and six pairs of oxen pulling eight logs along. It seemed slow work, but when we considered the size and number of logs we saw that they were accomplishing a good deal. A short time before a heavy log fell on the hindmost pair of oxen and killed them."

Will told Janette that she had better put cotton in her ears if she came near a "bull-whacker", who was the most important man in the lumberman's crew. His profanity was so mighty that when he began to swear, so the woodsmen said, the bark of the small fir trees smoked for a minute, then curled up and fell to the ground. If the stick and the swearing were not enough to speed up the oxen, the whacker might jump on the animals' backs and run the whole length of the team yelling.

Will also described this trip in one of a series of articles on "Impressions of Oregon," which he wrote under the pen name of Circumspectus for the *Valley Union* of West Chester, Pennsylvania.

In this article published March 21, 1885, he said:

"We had tried hard to get a top wagon, but failed. When we come to dodging under the fallen trees that lay across our way, in some instances, passing under one tree three times as it stretched down hill, across winding road, we were glad to have no top to shift. These forest giants do not seem half so tall us they stand side by side, but when fallen you see the reason for the oft repeated saying, 'You look three times before you see the top.' Some of the trees are eight and ten feet in diameter and the bark is 12 and 15 inches thick. It is beautiful wood and the entire mountain sides are wooded deep.

"Oregon scenery is grand and beautiful. The snow capped mountains which feed the refreshing streams, the abundant forests which are stored up as a national lumber-yard, are utilitarian in their aspect. But to the appreciative soul there are volumes which only the heart can read and interpret. Go read and be satisfied."

Again Janette wrote in her Diary:

"We had to wait from eleven o'clock until five for the steamer so we borrowed a fry pan and a pitcher and cooked over a camp fire our quail and trout and made lemonade. Then we rested and read until the 'Steamer Coos' came and we rode further up the bay to Marshfield. The bay was calm and the sunset light shone on the burnt timber on the mountain sides. The fresh young timber growing up reminding us how the child of today becomes the man of tomorrow.

"We were kindly welcomed by Mr. and Mrs. Bailey. We rested that night and on Friday afternoon the three men walked to Empire, four miles through the woods to engage a boat to have the next week. They rode back on the steamer. [The town of] Empire is in a boom, mills and houses being built by a Boston Company. Empire promises to be the Boston of the Pacific Coast, for there are many from that city there now. A hotel was burned there recently and another was brought down the river in a scow and set up in its place... The Boston Co., hope soon to have a minister all the time at Empire and Mr. B. thinks he may be the one selected.

"Saturday morning the men took a boat and went out to the mud banks and hunted clams. They stepped out of the boat into the mud. Will went in up to his knees, (he had rubber boots on). Sometimes they would stick fast and had to pull and tug to get each other out. Mr. L. lost his hat and running after it with great clogs of mud on his feet was no easy task, but a most amusing one to the others looking on.

"On Saturday evening a fresh English Episcopalian clergyman from Australia and the Sandwich Islands called. His accent and amusing manner of telling of his experiences kept us in a roar of langhter.

"The conversation turned on Chinese, he told of an instance when some Chinamen had been put in a boat with him. One was about to sit down beside him. The odor being strong, he said, 'You go over there, John, you don't fit.'

"Sunday morning, we attended service in the Academy building. The Episcopalian minister officiating, a neat little sermon on duty, little because the Litany consumed so much time. Good singing by the choir. In afternoon all attended S.S. but me. In the evening all attended service as the paper stated 'Divine Service by Rev. W. S. Young.' Some boys got up and started out during the sermon. Will stopped and waited. The stillness was oppressive, only broken by their steps on the stair. At close of service, we heard a great running down stairs and Mr. B. rose and said we need not be surprised to see the lights blown out in the hall as it was a frequent occurrence, and ended by quoting the words of the sermon, 'They loved darkness rather than light.'

"Monday morning we got things ready and were in the boat by eleven o'clock, by that time the tide was going out very fast and the Bay was rough. Every lurch made me fear the boat would go over. Mrs. B. was quite brave being used to the water, but I would be a long time getting over my terror. When we got in the river (Coos) it was another smoother going, although it was hard pulling against the tide. Soon it occurred to the men that they could use my shawl as a sail, so they had some fast sailing and some sport for a while.

"We went up the river 12 miles where we camped. The men took the boat and went on up the river to get milk, eggs, butter, bread and fruit from the farmers. They stayed so late, we were worried about them and frightened to be left so late. They were more worried on our account for there were two men in a boat somewhere near, whose actions seemed suspicious and Mr. B. knew them to be of doubtful character. Our men came about eight o'clock and it being too dark to have supper outside we went in the house. The men built a fire, some eggs were boiled though how they could eat in such a dirty cabin, I could not understand. The room was 10 × 12. The walls had once been papered but there were only a few shreds left. The floor was dusty, dirty and littered. The mantle piece and table likewise. The cupboard had no doors so dishes and sugar, salt, and lard, etc. were exposed to whatever came along. Boilers and pans looked uninviting. There were two beds, straw mattresses, plenty of blankets. Here and there lay a pipe made out of a potato with a stick stuck into it. On the table was a eucher deck and an eagle's claw.

"The disorder and the dirt were beyond description but the glow of the fireplace enlivened the scene with the addition of a supper. Soon we went to bed. We could not think of undressing in such a place, so slept with our clothes on. Mrs. B. and I had one bed. I slept soundly, but she passed a miserable night so did Mr. B. but Mr. L. and Will forgot themselves until morning. Mr. L. rose and went off by himself across the river, climbed the steep bank and hunted deer but with no success. We arose later, had breakfast, spent the day reading, hunting ferns, boating, fishing — thus the time passed, — but the deer would not show themselves, the fish would not bite, so in despair, the last day we made a net of towels and boated over to a spring and caught 77 wee fish, which made our supper. Supplies during the camping were obtained from the farmers.

"Thursday morning we started and after rowing four miles got back to Marshfield. The afternoon we spent baking, Mr. L. going to Sumner to bring wagon. On Friday morning we drove to Empire, six miles mostly through forests, in places through burnt timber. Drove on four miles to South Slough. Asked to be ferried over but the ferryman said the horses would have to swim across and the wagon be taken apart to get it on the little scow. We decided not to go, so hunted a place on the bank, had dinner. Then the men rowed across and saw so much game, ducks, eagles, etc. that they came for their guns, stayed over there till seven o'clock. The tide came in and they had a hard time getting back to the slough. We then harnessed

the team and went to a house that was empty for the time being. The family, Wilsons were absent but Mr. W. gave us
permission to stay all night. We ate our supper on the porch
and enjoyed the fine view of the bay and ocean, watched the
sun sink into the Pacific, watched a vessel being towed over
the 'bar' by a pilot, saw a pet fawn the Wilsons have.

"When bed time came we could not persuade ourselves
to get in the beds, so we built a fire in the parlor, got some
bed clothing and slept on the floor. We did very well though
Will kept the party awake talking about a flea that I whispered
to him that I had. The house was musty and cluttered and some-
what dirty which was not to be wondered at. Mrs. Wilson
had gone away for a drive, had found she was needed at her
daughter's so had been away for weeks. The parlor was
adorned with curious shells and mosses, two myrtle wood, home
made tables, etc. The kitchen had been left in a hurry. The
things from a meal in the cupboard, a little coffee, tea, some
milk (long soured) and on the table the invariable eucher deck.
I wonder in how many homes that game is played in Oregon.

"Next day we left there and all went to the beach. To get
down to it, we stopped at a house of a woman Mrs. Barker
living there whom Mr. B. knew. She used to bake for them.
We went down to the beach and got a great quantity of moss
and shells. Mr. B. and Will went away out on the pier which
the government is building and got six dozen star fish beautiful in color. We returned to Mrs. Barker's. The men went
back to Mr. Wilson's to get the team which they succeeded in
doing after a long time. Mr. L's horse was easily caught but
the other was a sly old horse and she would let them get so
near, then would back off. They tried for three quarters of
an hour. Mr. B. riding L's horse and Will with the oats. They
let down the bars and Mr. B. started down the road, she followed. Will was behind a bush to head her off. Mr. B. finally
turned and galloping back quickly, she turning and following.
Mr. Lockhard had by that time returned from the beach and
he caught her. Guess had she not been a borrowed horse she
would not have escaped a whipping.

"In the meantime Mrs. Barker had been kind, giving us
something to eat and giving us shells and moss and flowers,
and talking in her broken English (she is German) and making

a fuss over us and ejaculating frequently 'Mein Gott.' She told me she despised fleas. Went one day to a neighbor's, had to get up in the night to hunt for fleas. 'Ugh,' she said, she would always wear her drawers when she went again.

"We started at three o'clock, got back to Marshfield about dark, tired, very tired having been on the go all day. The beach along Barker's is called 'Rocky Point' and 'tis well named. We walked over rocks some of them with basin-shaped holes in them in which we found a peculiar jelly-like animal that on being touched closed up. The rocky bed was composed of petrified shells that sticking up cut our rubbers. 'Twas a curiosity bed to us, petrified shells and wood, curious shells, rock oysters and moss and we were loath to leave as we enjoyed the time there so much better than up the river. But our stay seemed short for we only had one more day."

On the next Sunday, Will preached a children's sermon after Sunday School in Empire. At a hotel they had a dinner more in Eastern style than anywhere else in Oregon. Among other delicacies were clam soup and fried clams. Mrs. Bailey and Janette did not go to church. They rested and talked and compared experience with Missionary Societies. Mrs. Bailey told her of one woman who used rough words, and was told that she couldn't use such language. She replied, "I ain't coming to no Society where you can't cuss nor nuthin." Janette told her of a man to whom Will had talked about swearing. He promised that he would stop. Then Will heard him say, "Jesus Christ," and took him to task. "Why, preacher, that ain't swearing," he remonstrated, "even you say that in church."

Janette's Diary continues:

"Monday noon, we left for Turner, drove to Coos City, got off our way once but by it got to see Newport the coal depot. At Coos we were towed across, first one horse at a time then the wagon and we went in a boat."

Will had read that the Coos Bay region was opened for settlement in 1855. There was little level land for the pioneers. But the waters were full of fish of every kind, and on its surface were ducks and geese. The beaches were packed with clams, and the woods were full of grouse and deer. The early inhabitants ate well.

Janette wrote of the trip back:

"We were told to stop at Bettis' all night. They were religious people. At nine o'clock got there, were kindly entertained and given fruit for our next day's journey. Saw a pet fawn much nicer than the one at Wilson's.

"Drove along all day only stopping for noon. Will and Mr. L. fished got three small trout. I gathered maiden hair fern and moss. The stage came along and told me about the Roseburg fire the night previous (18th August) hotel burned and owner and a Mr. Johansen of Astoria, many inmates were scorched but not seriously. 4 saloons and the post office were also burned.

"We rode on over the mountain. Mr. L. wanted to camp on summit but I would not agree so went on and it soon grew dark. We saw below us forest fires and soon came near to some few trees burning, one sending sparks in every direction, and near it we found one burnt off and lying across the road, being about 3 feet in diameter. We got out, I clambered over it and they took the wagon down a steep bank past it. Soon came to 19 mile house. I wanted to stay all night it was so dark, but soon changed my mind. They were retiring. Will called them up. A woman came out with a candle. Will said, 'Have you any antlers for sale?' 'Yes,' so he went in and we in the wagon could see all that went on. Soon a boy slipped out behind his ma with naught to cover him but a shirt that needed lengthening, he ran back and I saw another in like fix. They disappeared then came back standing where they thought they were screened, their curiosity making them unwilling to lose a word and put on their pants. We by this time had an audible smile. The woman left the men to select the antlers and slipped around to front porch and standing in the dark took inventory of us. We got three antlers for 75 cents.

"Rode on down mountain to toll gate. It is kept by a woman, she was not able or was afraid to come out, told us to go on to barn and pay man. Mr. L. went, could not make him hear, so on we drove. Got to 18 mile house, Mrs. Brown's by 9½ o'clock. Had a good sleep, breakfast of grouse, beef, eggs, butter, milk, oatmeal, etc. They gave me some ocean agates and large sugar pine cones. Will bought me a fawn skin tanned for 25 cents.

"Then the last day's ride began. It was hot dusty and disagreeable, such a change from mountain driving. The men ferried the team themselves across the Umpqua river. We camped in an oak grove near a house then drove on, hunting quail on the way. Took tea at Stranger's got to Oakland 9½ o'clock, tired and dusty, had breakfast early and took cars arriving at Turner at one o'clock, glad indeed after all our wanderings to be home. How these experiences make us love and appreciate our little home."

After their return on August 21, Janette made no entries in her Diary until September 16, when she wrote:

"On the afternoon of our arrival Will went out to catch Prince, but a 640 acre field was very much larger than he dreamed. After wandering around till dusk he went to house, they gave him a horse and he tried again with no success so he came home. Next morning. Walter Peacock came down and bought Prince. They went out into the field and after a long search found him. Will bought Mr. McIntosh's horse for $125. He is a fast traveller, can go to Salem eight miles, in forty minutes. Will is thankful he does not have to spend so much time on the roads."

When they returned home the fields were ripe for the harvest. The golden wheat and oats stretching out for miles made a beautiful sight. It showed how rich was the Willamette valley. Janette wrote of the harvesting:

"Sunday work is a great grievance to us. Nearly every farmer round here works the whole 7 days. There have been some worthy instances of sabbath keeping. Cole's had a big debate over the matter. Mr. C. taking sides with the threshers but Mr. Bowman and Mr. Cornelius and the women prevailed and the threshers went home. Even church members saw the matter only as a case of necessity and worked part or all of the day. Will went to Jefferson to preach September 14 and called at Mr. Longworth's, (Methodist minister) found him out in the field. He explained case of necessity, disappointed in getting thresher in clear weather and now the Lord had sent a little sunshine and they were making use of it. He had never worked on Sunday but once before. It seemed his wife had remonstrated to none effect. Threshing machines, mills etc., all were in operation on Sunday.

"Will preached at Turner September 7 on, 'Be sure your sin will find you out.'

"It was considered very applicable by many. Even between the sentences we heard the whistle of a thresher."

VIII. Unconquerable Love

During the early autumn, as the leaves were turning to gold and crimson and the weather was warm and dry, Janette felt more like her old self. Under the tall trees glowed the dogwood, and the scarlet vine-maple. The sumach's red spikes brightened the sides of the road and the leaves of the orchard trees fluttered down with every gust of wind. Janette gathered armfuls of goldenrod and purple asters, and put them in large earthenware crocks to decorate the church. She brought sprays of autumn leaves into the house, and from her garden picked colorful chrysanthemums grown from the slips that sister Fannie had sent her. They began to hope that their summer trip had benefited her. But when the rains began again, Janette's old cough came back.

On September 19 Janette and Will drove to Salem. They enjoyed the trip as the new horse, Duke, travelled so much faster than Prince. The wheat was nearly all threshed and the fields lay bare. On the way home a cold wind came up, and as Janette did not have a warm enough wrap she got thoroughly chilled. Will made her some hot tea and put her to bed. The next day she had a high fever and Will called the doctor. He gave her some medicine that helped her, but for a time she was quite ill. When she felt better she said that she would be always grateful to Dr. Parish, even if he did use long medical terms.

Will had to go to Presbytery and Synod, but he did not want to leave Janette alone. Mrs. Cole suggested that she stay with them, so they could take care of her while Will was away. She was well cared for at Coles, but while there she was shocked to hear lively piano music on Sunday. On October 14 she wrote in her Diary:

"Will enjoyed Presbytery and Synod. His S.S. paper on 'The Teacher's work outside of S.S.' and the one he gave at Synod, 'How to make our preaching more effective,' were considered helpful and also one he was called upon to deliver on 'Foreign Missions' before a popular evening audience (he had only a half day to prepare it.) My paper on 'How shall we more thoroughly enlist our churches in our special work' was liked and asked for publication.

"Will came home on evening train not waiting till close of Synod. Came and got team, drove Mr. Condit part way home, then back to Coles', stayed all night. Then we came down home and here I've been only doing the cooking. Only got house swept today, then by Will."

The Diary continues:

"Will went to Jefferson on Sunday... On his way home, Will got as far as Blakeneys when the horse being held in gave vent to his activity by lifting his feet into the air and landing with one on either side of the shaft, breaking it. He was frightened and broke into a run, but Will kept cool and held him checked. There were several ways in which he might have been thrown and hurt. God seemed very near to us in extending his protecting care to Will that day. Oh, how thankful I was. That with the long and tiresome ride and the preaching of Mrs. Hazleman's funeral service has been very wearing on Will, but help is given in every time of need."

On October 20 they drove to Salem. The leaves were gone from most of the trees and the skies were overcast. They heard the cries of the wild geese as they winged their way southward seeking sunshine. It made Janette wish that they could fly along with them. Years later Will wrote:

"During all this time Janette had never gotten used to the Oregon climate. There had scarcely been two months that summer without rain. Though under the care of Dr. R. who had the reputation of being one of Salem's best doctors, she was steadily running down in health and when we faced the question if there was not something more he could do, he said, 'No.' It is not medicine you need but you need more sunshine and a different climate and you would better go to S. Oregon or better still to Southern California."

On October 30 Janette wrote in her Diary:

"On the 30th there was an adjourned meeting of Presbytery for the installation of Rev. E. J. Thompson at Salem. We stopped at Mr. Van Eatons. We enjoy going there, it is in truth a Christian home. They earnestly strive to teach their little ones to do right in the fear of the Lord. Ethel, the oldest is a sweet child, so old fashioned and precise... Little Allie the boy is mischievous enough.

"I went to Doctor's and Will also had a conversation with

him and he advised a change for me to a dryer climate and named Southern Oregon or Southern California, but said not to go East because the change would be too great at this season of the year. We decided suddenly to leave here so as to get out of the dampness."

Will immediately went to the Reverend Robert W. Hill, who was probably the Stated Clerk of the Presbytery, and told him the circumstances. Mr. Hill wrote to the California Synod, recommending him as an excellent preacher and pastor. Mr. McDonald of the Los Angeles Presbytery answered immediately, mentioning several places: Riverdale (soon to be called Glendale), Boyle Heights and Pasadena. He added that the people are wanting a man with "innumerable gifts and graces." He hoped that the Lord would open up a field in that part of California, and offered his help cheerfully.

When Will came in with the letter he found Janette lying listlessly on the couch. "Oh, Will," she called, "I am so tired of this rain, rain, rain. How I do long for sunshine."

"Well, my love," he answered, "I have good news for you. Here is a letter from Los Angeles Presbytery accepting me, so soon we will be going to the 'land of sunshine,' where flowers bloom all the year round and you can have all the oranges that you can eat."

"How wonderful, Will. It is just what I have longed for. I will be truly sorry to leave these dear people, but I feel that in the warmer climate I will recover my health."

"I am sure of it, darling, and what is more, I promise you that next spring we will go back to Parkesburg for a visit."

"Oh, Will dearest, you are so good to me. I wish that you didn't have to leave your work, the churches you have organized and the opportunity for serving these dear people."

"Of course, dear, I am sorry to leave but nothing on earth means so much to me as to have you well again. We have felt from the first that we have been led by God's hand, and perhaps in Southern California there may be even greater opportunities for service."

The Oregon Presbytery hated to lose him, but realized his necessity for moving. Janette's Diary tells of those last days of parting with dear friends, selling their furniture and personal possessions:
October 30.

"I called a meeting of the Missionary Society to elect new officers ... We have thirty members now ... It was hard to meet and say 'Goodbye' to the ladies among whom I have labored for a year.   Afterwards some wanted to buy some little trinkets for remembrance.   One after another told us how much they would miss us.

"At Marion Sunday Will made the announcement for the first time and the people seemed so sorry.   Mr. Ford said he felt lonely for the first time in Marion.   Mr. Rutherford said he knew he could not be suited as well again.   One and another has said Will leaves without an enemy.   Well do we feel that the people have been very kind to us and have loved us and we shall not likely find as good cooperation again."

Little by little the furniture and household goods were sold, at a loss, but they were glad to dispose of them.   A newly-married couple were going to move into a little house text door.   They bought the walnut bedroom set, the kitchen stove, dining room table and the furniture in the study, but let Janette and Will continue to use them until they left, which made things much easier for them.

Janette's Diary tells of the horse:

November 1.

"Mr. McIntosh took his one hundred and twenty-five dollar horse back.   Will giving him twenty-five dollars for the use of it for three months!   Good pay for being well kept all the time!   Then Mr. McIntosh allowed the impression to go abroad that he magnanimously took the horse off Will's hands as an accommodation.   Oh! morality thou art a Jewel!"

It was the time of the Presidential elections of 1884.   Mrs. Cornelius, who was strong for women's rights, asked Will how he was going to vote.   He replied with a twinkle in his eye, "The way my wife tells me."   Mrs. Cornelius was horrified.   As Janette wrote in her diary, "Some people just can't take a joke."   Will knew that Janette's interest in Grover Cleveland was more because his father was a Presbyterian minister than for his political views.   Will was for the Republican candidate, James G. Blaine.   When Cleveland was elected, in the first Democratic victory since the Civil War, Janette was pleased that she had favored him.   "Some day, Will, we women will be able to vote."

Friends like Mrs. Rutherford and Mrs. Hilleary were especially kind.   Some brought in home-made cakes and bread and gifts.   Other friends came in to help pack the piano and all of Will's 550 books. They all said how much they would miss them, and that Sundays would never seem the same.   They were sure that no other minister would suit them so well.

In undated notes which William Stewart Young made many years later, about his work in Oregon, he said:

"The people were wonderfully kind and while the conditions were very primitive to what we had been used to, the generous kindness of the people gave us a home feeling.   The work prospered.   We were very diligent in calling and trying to get the people interested in attendance with the result that at Turner there were several who would attend quite regularly who really had no personal sympathy with or experience of vital faith.   So their chief interest was to discuss around the Drug Store fire the sermons and criticize keenly . . . The people in general were very appreciative of a pastor and most cordial in their welcome to their homes which in many instances were most humble and here and there most primitive.   But they were responsive and there was much encouragement in the work."

On November 2, 1884, they held their last service at the Octorara Church.   Will's register of sermons records that 150 persons were present.   This specially large turnout, to bid them farewell, was in striking contrast to the seven who had attended his first preaching there 15 months before.   Janette's Diary, written December 11 after they had reached Los Angeles, tells of this service:

"Our last day at Sunday School was a very precious one, the farewell meeting.   After Sunday School Will gave his last children's sermon and collected the money raised by the missionary gardens.   There were nine dollars and five cents.   Some of the children earned it by raising potatoes, corn, cabbage, and some by gathering eggs.   Will gave it to Mr. Hill for the Alaska Indians.

"As we were about to be dismissed, Mrs. Day, a good Baptist lady, rose and in a neat and touching speech referred to our work there and asked Will and me to stand together near the pulpit so that they could all shake hands with us and bid us 'Goodbye' while they sang:

'Shall we gather at the river
Where bright angel feet have trod;
With its crystal tide for ever
Flowing by the throne of God?

Ere we reach the shining river
Lay we ev'ry burden down;
Grace our spirits will deliver
And provide a robe and crown.
Soon we'll reach the silver river,
Soon our pilgrimage will cease,
Soon our happy hearts will quiver
With the melody of peace.
Yes we'll gather at the river,
The beautiful, the beautiful river,
Gather with the saints at the river,
That flows by the throne of God.'

"This was done with scarcely a dry eye in the house; well do we feel that the people have been very kind to us and have truly loved us."

As the congregation passed by they looked with sympathy and affection at the faces of their young minister and his wife. She had grown much thinner, the tell-tale spots of color burned in her cheeks, and her dark eyes seemed even larger. Her warm friendly smile, that had so won their hearts, was the same, only now it expressed more sympathy and understanding.

They could see Will's anxiety over his wife's health in the tender, protective way that he helped support her, with his arm about her slender waist. The people had grown to love them in the short year and a half that they had been in Turner. There was sadness in their hearts as they said farewell, and they were fearful of what the future might hold for Janette.

Janette and Will were to leave for Woodburn the next day for a farewell visit with their dear friends, the Voorhees. Their valises were packed. The house looked bare and lonesome with most of the furniture and their personal belongings moved out. Only their little study remained bright and cheerful with a good wood fire in the stove. Kind friends had brought in their supper. Now Janette lay on the couch exhausted after a hard day.

"Will, please read to me," she begged. He took up their well worn copy of Pilgrim's Progress, and read to her in his gentle, soothing voice. Then they talked of all that the year and a half in Oregon had meant to them. They reviewed some of their amusing experiences.

"Isn't it strange, Will dear," said Janette with a laugh, "The very things that bothered us when we first came here, such as every-one wanting to know all our affairs, endeared them to us when we realized it was just friendly interest."

"You know, darling," he replied earnestly, "all of our lives we shall treasure the memories of our days in Oregon."

On November 8 they sailed from Portland for San Francisco. Their ship was the *State of California,* which Janette said "is not the sturdy vessel she used to be, so they use her carefully." On the trip, "Will was not seasick but I was sick enough for two." From San Francisco they went to Los Angeles by train.

On December 11, Janette continued her **Diary:**

"When we reached Los Angeles and saw the bright sun-shine all day long and the trees and flowers as fresh as in summer we could not realize Christmas is near. How grateful I am for the warmth and light of the sun — it is already taking the chilliness out of me and making me feel stronger."

Their brief life together in California is another story. Janette's improvement in health was precarious. Entries in the diary became less frequent and more scattering. One of her friends, Mrs. M. D. Condit, wrote in the *Occident*:

"One by one Janette's duties dropped from her hands. Still she could plan and labor for her dear church and mission work. She was always cheerful, uncomplaining and gentle. She bade her friends express no regret as the struggle was all over with her heart. They knew that she was only lingering to hear the word of the Master, 'Come up higher'."

Death came to Janette, shortly after her 29th birthday, on October 26, 1887, quietly at eventide. "So He giveth His beloved sleep." Burial was in the cemetery of the Upper Octorara Church at Parkesburg, Pennsylvania.

Will ended the Diary in his own writing:

February 29, 1888.

"As I write tonight four months after, it all seems as fresh as though but yesterday . . .

"A few hours after her death . . . I walked out into the yard. The stars were shining beautifully but Oh! everything was so still. This world never seemed so quiet before. My faith pierced the stars it is true, but the beauty seemed gone and there I prayed to the God of Heaven and the God of my

dear Janette as I soliloquized alone! alone! alone! and asked
for strength to bear all and to glorify Him in the little while
that I linger. It didn't seem far up to Heaven but the way
seemed so silent and I longed to know the joys and glories
she had now learned and seen. To know only a small part of
what she had learned in the short time she had been within
the veil."

He closed with the words:

"The loved ones are not lost for love is eternal."

Envoi

William Stewart Young spent a busy and fruitful life in California following his arrival in Los Angeles in December, 1884.

As a pastor he was instrumental in establishing several churches. His first assignment was as supply pastor, both at Glendale and at Boyle Heights in Los Angeles. He helped buy for $100 the lot for the Glendale Presbyterian Church, of which there had already been a beginning. The new building was dedicated June 28, 1885. He organized the Boyle Heights Presbyterian Church May 3, 1885, and its new building was dedicated five months later. He was its pastor for 12 years. In January, 1897, he organized the Knox Presbyterian Church in the southern part of Los Angeles. He was its pastor for about ten years, and then became its pastor emeritus.

In church organization he held positions of prominence. For 40 years he was the Stated Clerk or chief executive officer, and Treasurer, of the Synod of California, from its beginning in 1892 to 1932. Also he was the Stated Clerk and Treasurer of the Presbytery of Los Angeles from 1897 to 1935. He served as Moderator of the Los Angeles Presbytery and of the Synod of California. He was a member of national bodies organized by the Presbyterian Church, and a leading authority on ecclesiastical law and procedure. Innumerable ministers and laymen came to him for the wise counsel for which he was so widely known.

Occidental College was one of his major interests. As a founder he called the meeting on February 15, 1886, which led to its organization in 1887 as "The Occidental University of Los Angeles." He was Secretary of the Board of Trustees from 1887 until his death 50 years later. In 1905-06 he was Acting President of the College.

The Hollenbeck Home for the Aged, one of the first and best-established homes of its kind, bore his imprint. Mrs. Elizabeth Hollenbeck, a charter member of the Boyle Heights church and widow of J. E. Hollenbeck, a founder of the First National Bank of Los Angeles, was moved to create this Home in memory of her husband. William Stewart Young was long a trustee of the Home, and from 1906 also became its superintendent until shortly before

his death.   He also was a founder and trustee of Monte Vista Grove
Homes of Pasadena, from its organization until his death.

Besides these major activities, he was a worker in numberless
good causes in the community.   He received honorary degrees from
Wabash College, Lafayette College (his alma mater), and Occidental
College.

On June 25, 1889, he was married to Adele Nichols, a graduate
of Mount Holyoke College, and a person of rare charm and ability.
She had taught in the Los Angeles schools and later became Secretary to the City Board of Education.   To them were born five children: Arthur, Paul, Walter, John and Sarah.   She was a popular
speaker and often conducted devotionals at women's meetings.   She
wrote for papers and magazines, and also words for occasional hymns
and other verses.   Rather than accept outside offices, she kept her
main interest in her home and family.   She was a constant help and
inspiration to her husband and a true helpmate in his work.

Both of them passed away in 1937, beloved by their children,
grandchildren and countless friends.

NOTE ON SOURCES

The main source is of course the Diary of Janette Lewis Young, in which at times William Stewart Young made entries. I have likewise drawn upon clippings pasted in the Diary, both of local items of news and of articles which he wrote for the *Valley Union* of West Chester, Pennsylvania, in 1885, on "Impressions of Oregon."

Also for contemporary data of that era in Oregon, and of train travel, I have drawn upon the following:

Adams, James Truslow, Album of American History, v. 3, 1853-1893, New York, circa 1946.

Allen, Horatio, The Railroad Era, New York, 1884.

Bancroft, Caroline, Colorful Colorado: The Colorado Tourist and Illustrated Guide to the Rocky Mountain Resorts, Denver, 1859.

Bancroft's Guide for Travellers by Railway, Stage and Steam Navigation in the Pacific States, No. 1, San Francisco, 1870.

Beebe, Lucius, High Iron, A Book of Trains, New York, 1938.

—, and Clegg, Charles, Hear the Train Blow, New York, 1951.

Board of Christian Education, Presbyterian Church, Presbyterian Panorama, Philadelphia, 1952.

Crofutt, George A., Crofutt's New Overland Tourist and Pacific Guide, Omaha and Denver, 1883.

Dall, Caroline H., My First Holiday, Boston, 1887.

Denver & Rio Grande Railway, Tourist Handbook, Denver, 1883.

Drury, Clifford M., Henry Harmon Spaulding, Caldwell, Idaho (The Caxton Printers), 1936.

—, Marcus Whitman, M. D., Pioneer and Martyr, *Ibid.*, 1940.

Graft, J. F., Graybeard's Colorado, Philadelphia, 1882.

Hudson, T., A Scamper Through America, 1882, E. P. Dutton, New York.

Husband, J., The Story of the Pullman Car, Chicago, 1917.

Illustrated Transcontinental Guide of Travel, the Atlantic to the Pacific Ocean, New York, n.d.

Lathrop, G. A., Little Engines and Big Men, Caldwell, Idaho (The Caxton Press), 1954.

Leslie, Mrs. F., California, A Pleasure Trip from New York to San Francisco, New York, 1877.

Frank Leslie's Illustrated Paper, Pike's Peak, Colorado, New York, 1871.

Lockley, Fred, Oregon's Yesterdays, New York, 1928.

—, Oregon Folks, New York, 1927.

McArthur, Lewis A., Oregon Geographic Names, Portland, 1883. Reprinted, Binfords & Mort, Portland, 1928.

Mencken, Augustus, The Railroad Passenger Car, Baltimore, 1957.

Nash, Wallis, There and Back, London, 1877.

—, Two Years in Oregon, New York, 1881.

Presbyterian Historical Society, Journal, Presbyterian Beginnings in Oregon, Philadelphia, 1947.

Shearer, F. E. (Ed.), The Pacific Tourist, New York, 1882.

Victor, Mrs. F. F., All Over Oregon and Washington, San Francisco, 1872.

Williams, H. T. (Ed.), The Pacific Tourist, New York, 1880.

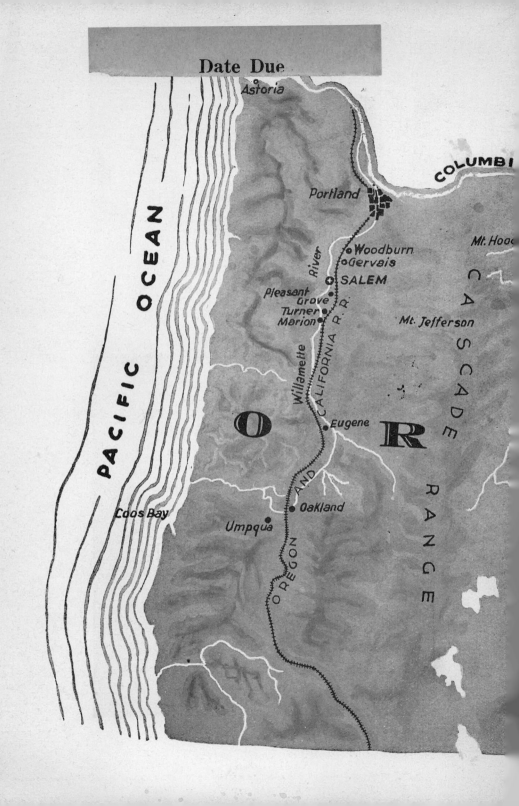